MASTERING THE ART OF CONCENTRATION

21 Hacks to Improve Your Focus

A Happy Thoughts Initiative

Mastering the Art of Concentration

21 Hacks to Improve Your Focus

By WOW Publishings Pvt. Ltd., India

ISBN : 978-81-989258-9-3

Published by WOW Publishings Pvt. Ltd., India

First edition published in July 2025

Printed and bound by Trinity Academy for Corporate Training Ltd, Pune

This book is based on the Hindi book titled, *Concentration - Ekaagra Mann ka Chamatkaar* by WOW Publishings Pvt. Ltd., India

To those,
who, like the ace archer Prince Arjuna,
are prepared for their concentration to be tested.

Content

APPENDICES

Preface

Make Work As Worship

Imagine how your favorite athlete would perform if they played with only 90% focus. Chances are, they would likely lose the match. Similarly, what if your teacher taught with a half-hearted effort? Your academic performance would undoubtedly suffer, and you would probably hold them accountable for it.

Now, consider your younger sibling studying with a distracted mindset, spending more time browsing the internet than focusing on their studies. Or envision a surgeon operating on a loved one with divided attention. Would you tolerate such a lapse in commitment in these critical situations?

Surely not! But are you giving your 100% attention to your work? Probably not. Then, how can you expect that from others? If you expect others to be fully committed to their work, you must practice the same.

Imagine if everyone performed their work with only 50% attention in every field; how would life be? Undoubtedly, they would face failure, frustration, and setbacks. On the other hand, if they performed their tasks with 100% focus, the quality of their work would improve, their productivity would rise, and they would be able to give due attention even to the minutest aspects of their tasks.

Since childhood, we have heard our parents and teachers repeatedly tell us, "Read carefully," "Pay attention while studying," and "Study with your heart and soul." While they urged us to study with concentration, neither they could explain it to us, nor could we grasp how to actually do it. Consequently, their well-intended words fell on deaf ears, and we ended up working in a distracted, unfocused manner.

However, if we truly understand the crux of concentration and work on it, it can create miracles in our lives. Let's understand it with a story.

> Once upon a time, God was passing by the Earth. As God walked past a mountain, He noticed a farmer with a chisel and hammer working to break through one side of the mountain. While toiling, the farmer prayed, "O God, help me break this mountain." God smiled and wondered, "How could this small man possibly break such a massive mountain? His prayers won't be answered, no matter how much he wishes for it."
>
> God approached the farmer in disguise and asked, "What are you doing?"
>
> The farmer replied, "I am a farmer. My fields are on this side of the mountain, but the mountain blocks the rain. The clouds collide with it, and the rain falls on the other side, leaving my fields dry and barren. Hence, I am trying to break through the mountain."
>
> God thought to Himself, "Poor man! He is investing his energy into an impossible task. What can he accomplish with just a chisel and hammer? The mountain will never budge."
>
> As God continued on His way, He heard the mountain plead, "O Lord, please protect me! This man intends to break me; he will bring an end to my existence." God responded, "Don't worry. This little farmer alone won't be able to harm you. He

will tire out in a day and give up." With this reassurance, God moved on.

However, a few days later, when God passed along the same path, He was astonished to see that the mountain was more than half broken. The farmer was no longer alone; many other farmers had joined him in his efforts to break the mountain. The mountain cried in sorrow and despair, "O Lord, I told You that this man would destroy me. Look at what he has achieved in such a short time!"

God asked in disbelief, "But how did this happen?" The mountain replied, "My Lord, although he is a humble farmer, he possesses the extraordinary power of focus and concentration. This is a rare gift that only a few possess. Yet, whoever has it can move mountains as large as me!"

When someone is fully engrossed in their work, all their senses work together cohesively, creating a single-minded focus on the task at hand, rendering them oblivious to their surroundings. Their concentration is so intense that they forget about hunger and thirst. When their concentration reaches its peak, i.e., at 100%, their body, mind, heart, emotions, and thoughts align, transforming the work into an act of devotion.

That is the incredible power of concentration! Though invisible, those who possess it can move the largest mountains and achieve seemingly impossible tasks. This power is not a physical strength that can be developed by going to the gym, building muscles, or following a diet. It is the power of the mind, nurtured by training the mind through consistent practice, shielding it from distractions, and providing it with proper understanding.

In today's fast-paced world, everyone looks for quick and easy ways to get things done more efficiently. You may have heard the term "hack," which refers to techniques designed to help complete tasks faster and with less effort, such as kitchen hacks, fashion hacks, home organization hacks, gadget hacks, and more.

People turn to these hacks to simplify their daily lives. In this book, we will explore 21 hacks to improve focus. By adopting these seemingly simple hacks and practicing them consistently, we can improve our concentration in a short time and achieve better results.

I

What is Concentration?

To achieve success in any task, focus is essential. Those who work with a scattered mind can never realize the value of success in a hundred years.

~ Swami Vivekananda

Everyone knows that we should perform every task with concentration. But what exactly is concentration, what is its fundamental nature, and what characterizes this state of mind?

The word "Concentration" originates from the Latin word "Concentratio." It refers to the act of bringing things together, whether physically or mentally, into a single place. Essentially, it emphasizes the importance of directing focus toward a singular pursuit, whether it is work, reading, or a personal goal, while setting aside everything else.

Let's explore the fundamental nature of concentration through the story of Prince Arjuna from the Indian epic, the *Mahabharata*.

> Dronacharya was a master archer and a revered teacher of warfare to both the Kaurava and Pandava princes. He wanted to test the archery skills of his students. He placed a wooden bird atop a tall tree and asked them to strike its eye. However, before allowing them to shoot, he asked each of them what they saw. Some saw

the bird, others saw the tree, and still others saw the sky. When it was Arjuna's turn, he replied, "I see only the eye of the bird." Thereafter, with his steady gaze fixed only on the eye of the bird, Arjuna shot his arrow and pierced the target perfectly.

This demonstrates how Arjuna's extraordinary power of concentration helped him achieve his goal. When he aimed at the bird's eye, he focused solely on it, disregarding everything else around him. This exemplifies the fundamental nature of concentration. When engrossed in a singular pursuit, we become oblivious to our surroundings. All our senses, including our eyes, ears, mind, and intellect, become fully absorbed in that activity, forgetting everything else around us. This remarkable power of concentration allows us to become so deeply immersed in the task that we can barely perceive anything beyond it.

Swami Vivekananda was one of the greatest thinkers and philosophers in India. He was a devout follower and chief disciple of the 19th-century saint Sri Ramakrishna Paramhansa. He beautifully articulated the power of concentration in one of his famous quotes: "The powers of the mind are like the rays of the sun. When they are concentrated, they illumine." He eloquently compared the power of a focused mind to that of the sun's rays converging at a single point. Just as the sun's scattered rays can be concentrated using a convex lens to ignite a fire, a mind focused on a singular purpose can illuminate our lives with happiness, prosperity, and success.

However, when the mind loses focus, it becomes scattered in different directions and repeatedly changes goals like shifting sands. Unsure of how to prioritize tasks, while working on one task, it often thinks of other tasks or anticipates the outcome of the current task. In such a state, it dissipates energy in vain and weakens. It cannot perform any task properly, on time, or efficiently. Consequently, tasks performed with a half-hearted mind do not yield the desired outcome.

Let's explore the difference between a focused mind and a scattered mind using the example of Akhil and Rahul.

> Twelve-year-old Rahul was attending an online class at home. The teacher was teaching history, and Rahul was listening to her with his headphones on. However, his mind wandered in different directions, far from the lesson. Whenever a notification popped up on his mobile phone, he would start looking at it. A sudden ring of the doorbell further distracted him as he wondered, "Who could have come at this time? Did someone open the door?" Then, after a while, he became distracted by the enticing aromas wafting from the kitchen, thinking, "What's Mom cooking for breakfast today? It smells like pizza."
>
> Although he listened to the teacher, he barely grasped anything because his mind was scattered. He was waiting for the class to end so he could mark his attendance and close his laptop. He had already decided to read the chapter from the book later.
>
> Suddenly, the teacher asked him, "What did you understand from today's lesson?" Caught off guard by the teacher's unexpected question, Rahul went blank. He had not anticipated the teacher asking him a question. He was speechless and

> struggled to recall what he had learned. He kept looking down with his head bowed.
>
> Another student, Akhil, attended the same online class. He needed to prepare a presentation on the same topic for the next day, so he listened to the lecture attentively. He also faced the same distractions as Rahul but remained undeterred. Although breakfast being prepared in his kitchen, he didn't pay attention to it. He was so engrossed in the lesson that he remained oblivious to his mother entering and exiting his room, the doorbell ringing, and the passage of time. He was completely focused on understanding the topic being taught in class. After Rahul, when the teacher asked Akhil to summarize his learning, he effortlessly recalled the lesson and explained it step by step.

What differentiates Akhil from Rahul, resulting in their contrasting levels of concentration? It is a sense of purpose. Akhil needed to prepare a presentation on the same topic, so he listened to the lecture with rapt attention, while Rahul had no such purpose. He believed he could read the lesson from the book later if he didn't grasp it during the lecture. Thus, when there is a concrete reason or goal, the mind can concentrate more easily and effectively.

Like Rahul, we are caught up in numerous pursuits throughout the day. We spend a great deal of unproductive time with friends and relatives, but struggle to say "no" to them. We engage in many activities, knowingly or unknowingly, that often fail to yield fruitful results. We hoard countless items that no one will ever use. Consequently, when our focus is divided among multiple activities, our energy gets scattered into small parts. As a result, we find it challenging to concentrate fully on any single task.

Now, we need to gather our scattered minds. For this, we must set out on the path of single-mindedness and train our minds to concentrate. Consequently, the mind will stop chasing trivial pursuits like a horse without reins and stay focused. A focused mind leads to a successful life characterized by simplicity, peace, and serenity. It has the ability to elevate life to greater heights.

Many examples in nature demonstrate that scattered energy, when converged in one place, reaches its peak potential and fosters innovation. When sunrays are concentrated, they produce solar energy, which in turn generates electricity. Electricity is also generated by storing water in one location. When scientists work with a focused mind, new inventions emerge.

Concentration is a vital quality that should be prioritized. Without it, you may struggle to complete your work properly and ultimately fail to achieve the desired results. However, by making it a habit and incorporating it into your life, you can succeed in any task you undertake. Therefore, cultivate the habit of concentration, ensuring that even in the absence of a strong reason, your mind does not wander.

II

The Importance of Concentration

The shortest way to do many things is
to do only one thing at once.

~ Samuel Smiles

Once, in a distant village, a farmer embarked on a quest for water and decided to dig a well in his field. Despite his earnest efforts, his initial attempts yielded no water, leaving him disheartened. Undeterred, he began digging at another location, only to face the same arid outcome. He continued his search tirelessly, digging at different spots, yet each attempt brought only disappointment. As his fruitless labor stretched on, a heavy sense of dejection settled over him.

One day, he confided in a village elder about his struggle. The elder understood the farmer's plight and advised, "You've dug several pits, each only 6 to 7 feet deep. Instead of moving from one spot to another, you should have persisted and dug 6 to 7 feet deeper at the same spot every day. You lacked patience and gave up after merely scratching the surface. Now, focus your efforts on one spot and keep digging deeper until you hit water. Success is bound to follow."

Taking the elder's advice to heart, the farmer began digging at the same spot each day with focused effort. After reaching a depth of 20 to 30 feet, he finally struck water. Overwhelmed with gratitude, he thanked the old man for his guidance.

This example illustrates the importance of concentration and the miracles it begets. We often juggle between multiple tasks, intending to complete them all, only to leave them unfinished halfway. This depletes our time and drains our energy, making it difficult to complete any task effectively. Instead of working on many tasks, we must dedicate our time, effort, and focus to completing one task at a time. This approach enhances the likelihood of finishing tasks on time with better results. When we pursue any task with unwavering focus, success is assured. No matter what we do, concentration is essential.

Let's briefly explore the areas where concentration plays an important role.

1. **Achieve academic success:** Concentration is essential for achieving academic success, whether you are a first–grade student or pursuing a Ph.D. By studying with a focused body, mind, and intellect, you can gain a deeper understanding of the subject and retain knowledge more effectively over a longer period.
2. **Excel in sports:** Concentration is a significant milestone for anyone aspiring to excel in sports. To succeed in any competition, athletes must consistently practice their game with an unwavering focus to refine their skills. Without concentrated effort, it becomes nearly impossible to endure the challenges of competition.
3. **Pursue career aspirations:** In today's fast-paced world, staying updated with the advancements in your field is crucial for career growth. By cultivating focus in professional endeavors and discerning the most efficient paths and resources to achieve career aspirations, you can navigate your professional journey with confidence and ease.

4. **Attain desired goals:** Taking time to contemplate, i.e., engaging in deep and focused thinking before starting a task, broadens our intellectual horizons. Intuition serves as a guiding force as we create a mental plan or roadmap for the task. According to Pareto's 80-20 principle, dedicating 20% of our effort to focused thinking and planning can streamline the remaining 80% of our workload. This careful contemplation and planning significantly improve the overall quality of the work.

5. **Improve work quality and efficiency:** The success of any task or project hinges on careful planning, which requires focused effort. It also involves gathering diverse inputs from others through consultations or meetings and making decisions based on a thorough assessment of all possible outcomes, ensuring that quality remains paramount.

6. **Balance personal life:** As we invest our hearts in achieving our aspirations, we cannot overlook the intense competition across various fields. Whether in academics, sports, profession, or business, even a minor diversion of focus can result in missed opportunities, making unwavering concentration essential. However, concentration encompasses more than just activities in the workplace or marketplace. It also involves household responsibilities such as housekeeping, managing finances, and meal preparation. Imagine the flavor of food prepared without care. The key is to prioritize tasks effectively and establish a harmonious balance in all areas of life.

7. **Learn and understand a topic in depth:** You cannot grasp any subject without concentration. Concentration is the art of honing the mind to such precision that it remains focused on a single point, much like the tip of a needle. This involves aligning our internal and external senses to concentrate on one point while executing the task. Once fully focused, it becomes easier to explore the subject in depth. Concentrated

thinking enables one to unravel complex puzzles or problems with greater ease.

When we concentrate our body, mind, and intellect on accomplishing a task, we gradually begin to notice its finer details, and this attention to detail leads to high-quality outcomes.

To cultivate the habit of working with concentration, it is crucial to identify and eliminate the obstacles that hinder focus. By recognizing distractions and employing strategies to enhance concentration, we can boost our productivity. We will explore these strategies in the upcoming chapters.

III

External Factors That Weaken Concentration

Concentration is my motto - first honesty, then industry, then concentration.

~ Andrew Carnegie

Imagine stepping into your room and seeing your younger brother, Vishal, hunched over a jigsaw puzzle. Frowning in frustration, he tries to force a piece into the puzzle, but it stubbornly resists. He flings the piece aside with an exasperated huff, inadvertently sending a cascade of jumbled pieces scattering across the room.

"This puzzle is impossible!" He exclaims, upon seeing you. "See, none of the pieces fit together. I've been trying for a long time. Will you help me?"

Seeing his struggle, you offer to assist. "Alright, let's solve it together. But first, we need to gather all the pieces you've scattered around. As long as they are spread out, it'll be harder to find the right ones. It'll be much easier to solve the puzzle if we get everything in one place."

Vishal quickly gathers all the pieces into a pile and settles beside you to watch as you begin solving the puzzle. He patiently observes until you encourage him to take the lead. This time, he focuses intently on one empty space. Meticulously scanning the nearby pieces, he picks one and tries to fit it into the puzzle. Frustration flickers across his face as he raises his hand, ready to discard the mismatched piece. But he pauses, choosing instead to keep it within reach, determined to find a rightful place for each piece. He realizes that scattering the pieces around and constantly getting up to select one disrupts his focus, slows him down, and makes him frustrated and irritated. Like Vishal, we too need to delve deeper and understand the causes that weaken our ability to focus.

The following are the top five external factors that hinder our concentration.

1. **Electronic devices:** The digital world, comprising mobile phones, tablets, computers, and social media apps like WhatsApp, Telegram, Email, Facebook, Instagram, Twitter, YouTube, etc., can easily draw and distract us. Our lives now revolve around mobile phones, as they have seamlessly integrated into our daily routines and have become indispensable. While they simplify many of our tasks, our minds have become more distracted due to their excessive use. When the mobile phone is in our hands, it becomes challenging for our minds to concentrate on a single topic.

   For instance, when we start a new task, we typically begin by gathering relevant information on mobile phones or computers. However, while browsing this information, we don't even realize when we unknowingly visit some other irrelevant websites and waste our time. As a result, we take more time to complete our tasks, which hampers our productivity.

2. **Insufficient sleep:** Not getting enough sleep makes us less alert and focused, thereby impairing our cognitive function and diminishing mental sharpness. Consequently,

it becomes difficult to focus on anything, affecting both concentration and memory.

Mobile phones can also be a major reason behind insufficient sleep. Late-night gaming, music, social media, chatting, or binge-watching shows keep us glued to our screens. We must consciously reduce these activities, set clear boundaries, and prioritize timely sleep. Otherwise, chronic sleep deprivation will harm our health, cognitive abilities, and memory.

3. **Inadequate physical activity:** Regular exercise keeps us energized throughout the day, while skipping it can drain our energy levels. A lack of adequate physical activity often leads to tense and stiff muscles, which can cause restlessness and impair concentration. Prioritizing physical activity is essential for overall well-being. An adequate amount of physical activity keeps the mind active and focused, thanks to the boost in energy levels.

4. **Dietary habits:** If we fail to provide our brain with essential nutrients, we can experience fatigue, weakened memory, and diminished concentration. Consuming heavily processed food high in saturated fats notably impairs our ability to focus. In contrast, essential fatty acids are crucial for optimal brain function. Saturated fat-laden food fails to provide the necessary nutrients, leading to hunger, cravings, and overall malaise. To keep the mind and brain sharp and active, prioritizing a well-balanced diet is imperative. Optimal brain and mental health fuels sustained focus and productivity at work.

5. **Environmental factors:** Weather conditions, the surrounding environment, and our prevailing mood significantly influence our concentration. While noisy surroundings can disrupt our focus, some people find it difficult to focus even in a quiet environment. Whether there is noise or silence in the outside environment, if the

turmoil in our mind subsides and tranquility prevails, we can easily concentrate.

These are some of the factors that affect our concentration, which often go unnoticed. If we are working in a noisy environment and are unable to focus, we immediately complain and blame the noise for disrupting our focus. However, the factors mentioned above gradually hamper our ability to concentrate, and it takes time to repair the damage they caused.

The good news is that we can eliminate some of these distractions. We can reduce the overuse of mobile phones, ensure restorative sleep to give our brains adequate rest, minimize stress, maintain balanced energy levels with a proper exercise routine, and nourish our brains with nutritious food. Consequently, our ability to concentrate will boost, making it easier to achieve our goals. However, some internal factors also disrupt our concentration. We will explore them in the next chapter.

IV

Internal Causes of Poor Concentration

A mind that can concentrate attains complete stability.
A happy mind is a concentrated mind.

~ The Buddha

Whether you are a student, a homemaker, or a corporate executive, focus is essential for better performance. However, in today's fast-paced world, staying focused has become a significant challenge for many. Then how can we cultivate this vital skill? How can we train our mind to stay focused?

In the previous chapter, we explored the external factors that affect our focus. In this chapter, we will explore three key internal causes that contribute to an unfocused mind.

1. Lack of interest

Everyone has good concentration, but only in specific areas, which is referred to as selective concentration.

For instance, a woman is captivated by a telemarketing show that is showcasing a myriad of products. Another woman avidly searches for grab-on shopping deals on handbags, footwear, apparel, accessories, etc. Hours pass, but their focus remains unwavering. A third homemaker enjoys experimenting with new recipes. She tirelessly works toward refining her dishes to perfection. However, if you were to ask them to watch a science fiction show, none of them would be able to focus on it, as they wouldn't be interested in it.

Children often complain, "We can't concentrate on our studies." Yet when given a mobile phone to play games, they are glued to it for hours without interruption. If you turn on their favorite cartoon shows, their concentration peaks.

Many older people also lament their inability to concentrate, yet they remain completely absorbed for hours in a cricket or football match, showing no signs of distraction.

Thus, everyone has good concentration skills, but only in areas of interest to them. They often struggle to concentrate on topics that do not interest them. If we carefully observe, we will notice that concentration is most needed in boring activities. If one can focus well even on boring activities, they demonstrate good concentration skills.

2. Lack of goals

People often fail to understand why they perform certain activities, their goals, and what they aim to achieve by doing so.

Students often ask their parents, "What's the big deal about studying? Some of the most successful people were dropouts, yet they built massive business empires without formal education. What will I gain from studying?" While these questions are common, students often overlook the deeper rationale behind learning various subjects.

The human brain is akin to a supercomputer and studying various subjects catalyzes its development. While Mathematics fosters analytical skills, science enhances reasoning abilities. Languages and music nurture effective communication and expression. Each subject plays a vital role in the overall development of the brain. Students who fail to grasp this purpose often find subjects mundane, leading to diminished concentration.

Activities in schools are planned with a broader goal in mind. There is an aim beyond aim. When a child spends focused 5 hours in school each day, it lays the foundation for productive 8 hours in their future careers. The school serves as a training ground for honing essential skills. A child's confidence grows when they raise their hand to answer questions or engage in discussions. Likewise, participating in sports develops competitiveness and resilience, while making friends cultivates vital social skills.

You may have seen a sunflower. It exemplifies an important principle. Its whole and sole goal is the sun. It steadfastly follows the sun's path from east to west. It aligns itself with the sun's light and warmth. At dawn, it faces east and gradually turns west by evening. Similarly, aligning ourselves with a clear goal or direction illuminates our journey and assures a brighter future. Defining a life goal enriches our present experiences and positively reshapes our future. With a clear life goal, focus naturally follows, guiding us toward a brighter tomorrow.

Let's understand the importance of a goal with an example.

> Imagine a match between two teams. The players from both teams gathered on the field while warming up. Soon, their coaches joined them. The first team's coach instructed his players, "Run fast and make full circuits of the ground." Hearing this, his team members immediately started running.
>
> The second team's coach instructed his team, "You need to complete 10 laps around this field, so start now."
>
> The first team didn't know how many circuits they had to complete and when to stop. As a result, after completing 2 circuits, they got so tired that they couldn't run further. In contrast, the second team stopped only after completing 10 rounds.
>
> Why was there such a distinct contrast in their energy levels and responses?

It was mainly because of the instructions given to them. The first team was instructed to run without knowing how long they needed to continue. Without a precise goal, they felt disoriented and drained as they struggled to find purpose in their actions. Consequently, they were tired after just 2 laps and claimed they couldn't run any longer. In contrast, the second team's energy stemmed from the clear understanding of their goal. This clarity allowed them to channel their efforts efficiently and pace themselves accordingly. So, they persevered until they achieved their goal and stopped only after completing their target of 10 laps.

Take a moment to reflect on your goals. If your concentration is poor and you cannot focus on your work, it implies that you lack clarity about the purpose of that work and the goal behind it. Therefore, before starting any task, ask yourself, "What is the goal of this task?" Once the goal is clear, your concentration will automatically improve.

3. Speed of mind

Our mind constantly oscillates between the past and the future. Sometimes, it spends hours dwelling on past events or imagining what lies ahead. Sometimes, it is consumed by regrets from the past or overwhelmed by anxieties about the future. As a result, it cannot remain in the present.

Due to this continual back and forth between reminiscing and anticipating, on average, around 50,000 to 60,000 thoughts run through our mind each day, reflecting the speed of our mind. But despite so many thoughts, how many tasks do we perform each day? At most 10 to 12. This means only 10 to 12 thoughts should suffice for these tasks. Unfortunately, that's not the case.

The human mind is a bundle of incessant thoughts, making it difficult to concentrate on the task at hand. For instance, when faced with an undesirable event early in the morning, we may find ourselves brooding over it all day. Similarly, disputes or arguments replay in our mind, trapping us in an endless loop. As a result, when we try to tackle any new task that requires mental clarity, our preoccupation with these incessant, repetitive thoughts hinders our ability to focus. This surplus of thoughts creates a bottleneck, much like a traffic jam, in our mind. Consequently, we often struggle to achieve our desired goals despite our inherent ability to perform tasks proficiently.

21 HACKS TO IMPROVE FOCUS

Use your intuitive mind, well-tuned body,
and a discerning intellect to accomplish tasks.
All achievements of life and occult powers
are the miracle of a focused mind.

1

Make Work Fun

Keep your mind on the things you want and off the things you don't want.

~ Hannah Whitall Smith

Imagine if you told a subject like Mathematics, "Hey, Maths, if you become interesting, I can understand you better." Would that be possible?

If you tell your boss, "If you make an interesting presentation, only then can I fully concentrate on this project." Would the company operate like that?

Is it right to tell the world, "You become interesting because I can't concentrate otherwise?" Or should we take up the responsibility of cultivating interest in that work?

Indeed, instead of finding inherently interesting work, we should explore ways to cultivate interest in the tasks we have, whether they are domestic chores, office tasks, or academic studies. Then work can become enjoyable, and we can easily focus on it.

Consider athletes, after spending hours perfecting their game and skills, they do not say, "I am exhausted." But when it comes to work, most people feel drained within a couple of hours.

Why does this happen? What is the difference between play and work?

If we carefully evaluate, we will realize that playing any sport inherently brings joy and entertainment. Therefore, people rarely complain of fatigue. Then why not make our work as enjoyable and engaging as our favorite sport? By doing this, we will not only feel happier but also become more productive.

Let's explore how we can make work interesting.

> A trainer had to commute 20 to 25 kilometers every day to reach his training venue. Despite his passion for training, he found the long commute incredibly boring and stressful. To make matters worse, the scorching heat and heavy traffic only intensified his frustration.
>
> One day, he wondered, "How can I make this journey fun?" He reflected on the kind of commute he would prefer and the facilities he would use to upgrade the level of enjoyment in the journey.
>
> After careful thinking, he went to the market and bought a nice pair of sunglasses. Then, he kept some fruit juice and a few packets of nuts in the car. Additionally, he loaded his pen drive with a melodic playlist to enjoy some soulful music during the drive. With this preparation, he was super excited to begin his journey.
>
> Now, while commuting, every time the car stopped at the red signal, he would sip some juice and nibble on some crunchy nuts. The soothing melodies of his favorite tunes played as his driving companion, turning the whole experience into a symphony of joy. As a result, he arrived at his training venue with a bright smile on his face. His uplifted mood not only made the journey enjoyable but also enhanced the learning experience, making it all the more enriching.

Like the trainer in the above example, we sometimes feel bored with our mundane activities and are least interested in them. We may find ourselves procrastinating on tasks that we resist or avoid, which in turn hampers our productivity and efficiency. On the other hand, when working on an activity of interest, we feel motivated to work for long hours and finish it fast with full concentration and quality. As a result, our productivity soars, and we achieve exceptional results with ease. The key, then, lies in making tasks more engaging and captivating.

So, from now on, let's commit to making our work more exciting and engaging to sustain our interests. Let's start by creating a list of tasks that usually feel monotonous. Whenever you encounter them and feel the urge to procrastinate, immediately counter it by saying, "Let's make it interesting." With this proactive approach, work will become fun, and you will feel motivated and focused to finish it quickly.

Enhance concentration playfully

We should learn the art of making work interesting like a game. However, some take even sports and entertainment seriously and consider serious matters trivial. For instance, some parents find playing with their kids a chore, especially when they are busy or don't feel like playing.

Similarly, some people watch sports with such intensity that their entire existence hinges on the outcome of the game. Their minds are consumed with the pressure of which team will win, and which team will make it to the finals. Paradoxically, these sports enthusiasts often ignore serious real-world issues. They may even mock or dismiss important global matters with laughter and frivolity. Ironically, their dedication to sports can escalate to alarming levels. If their favorite team suffers a defeat, it can trigger fury, leading to destructive actions like smashing their TV sets in fits of rage. They need to recognize that, ultimately, it is just a game and not worth such extreme reactions.

Some people watch their missed web series during the weekend, downplaying their other responsibilities. Instead, they should redirect that same passion and focus toward making their work as captivating as the entertainment thrills them, thereby boosting their concentration and productivity.

Now, we need to take sports with sportsmanship and also make work fun. You may wonder how this is possible. But it is indeed possible! There is no work in the world that cannot be made interesting. With determination, even the most boring work can be made enjoyable. With a little effort and a touch of creativity, we can breathe new life into our routine tasks and rediscover joy in the ordinary. We can fulfill our responsibilities, much like approaching a game with enthusiasm and focus.

Let's understand this with an example.

> A woman acknowledges the importance of exercise, yet doesn't find it interesting enough to start working out. Then, she adopts a creative approach to make it interesting.
>
> Using her imagination, she transports herself to a peaceful village setting. She imagines pulling water from a well with the bucket tied to a rope, feeling the resistance and weight of the imaginary load. After about 5 to 6 repetitions, she visualizes lifting a full bucket of water and pouring it into another container.
>
> As she progresses, she leans forward to grab the rope, bends to lift the bucket, and raises her hands to pour the water, effectively engaging her hands, core, and back muscles.
>
> To add variety, she incorporates torso twists, imagining herself tying a rope or swaying her hands back and forth. Further, she envisions juggling fruits or catching a virtual ball, infusing her workout regime with a creative flair. By sculpting different muscle groups through imaginative exercise, she transforms her boring regimen into a vibrant tapestry of different activities, turning the mundane into something engaging.

Similarly, we can transform our boring tasks into engaging ones, which will allow us to focus better and, as a result, increase our efficiency and productivity.

2

Employ Both – the Left Brain and Right Brain

Arise, awake, and stop not until the goal is achieved.

~ Swami Vivekananda

If we examine the structure of human anatomy, many parts of the body have left and right counterparts, such as our eyes, ears, hands, legs, kidneys, lungs, and more. Intriguingly, our brain, while singular, is also functionally divided into two parts—the left brain and the right brain.

The brain, although small, is one of the most vital organs of the human body, holding immense potential. It is the epitome of complexity, yet a marvel. It orchestrates all the body's activities, from voluntary actions performed consciously, like walking, sitting, eating, and talking, to involuntary functions that occur without our awareness, such as blinking, breathing, heartbeat, blood circulation, blood pressure regulation, sleep-wake cycles, hunger, digestion, and hormone secretion. Despite being such a crucial organ, the shocking reality is that we do not explore its full potential.

It is seen that most people use the right side of their body more than the left, but their left brain is used more. This stems from the interesting fact that the right brain controls the left side of our body while the left brain controls the right side. Each part of the brain has its own distinct role, and we can harness them to enhance our creativity.

While individuals with a dominant left brain excel in numerical skills, language, logic, and analytical thinking, those with a dominant right brain are more inclined toward artistic abilities, intuition, and creativity. People who predominantly use their right brain become deeply absorbed in their artistic pursuits and exhibit unparalleled concentration. You may have also observed that artists become so engrossed in their work—whether painting, sculpting, or composing music—that they are unaware of their surroundings. During these moments of deep work, their concentration reaches its peak, and they become one with their work.

Another distinctive trait of the right brain is the ability to conjure up scenes or objects that are not physically present. While imagining these scenes, we become disconnected from the outside world and focus entirely on visualizing them in our inner eyes, transporting ourselves into a different realm. This is another facet of concentration that allows us to perceive even non–physical things, creating a vibrant inner world beyond the confines of our tangible existence.

Let's understand how we can harness the traits of our left brain and right brain to increase our concentration.

Using the left brain

Sometimes, a task or project appears overwhelmingly huge and challenging to finish at first glance. This causes jitters, and we lose interest in doing the task. It hinders our concentration. In such situations, we can use our left brain. It helps us with numerical skills, articulate our creative thoughts in line with our vision, logically reason out solutions, and systematically organize them to bring them into action.

We can divide or break down tasks into smaller, more manageable parts and assign them to suitable people. This not only makes the work interesting but also facilitates easier completion. When the work is split into small tasks, concentrating on them becomes easier.

Let's understand this with the example of Suresh.

Suresh was a bright, talented student who actively participated in extracurricular activities. When his college held its annual concert, he was entrusted with complete responsibility for the event. Not only did he have to accomplish a huge task list, but he also needed to prepare and send invitations to approximately 4000 people, including VIP guests and college alumni, within a week. Suresh felt overwhelmed by the enormous scale of the task, and his anxiety soared. "How will I finish all this—printing, enveloping all letters, and writing each address? It feels like a never-ending task!" His stress peaked, making it difficult to focus.

But just then, Suresh took a deep breath and paused for a while. He decided to split the task and seek help from his friends. He spoke to his friends and divided the tasks into smaller groups. Within a week, the letters were printed and sealed in envelopes, addresses affixed, and invitations dispatched. What seemed like an insurmountable challenge was accomplished in just a few days. With clear explanation and effective coordination, his friends were able to focus on smaller jobs, collectively achieving a seemingly impossible feat.

Using the right brain

While performing mundane tasks at work, one loses interest and concentration. At such times, the right brain plays a vital role in making it interesting so that it can hold our focus. Work can be simplified by integrating creativity and imagination with our innate abilities, transforming its accomplishment into an exciting and joyful experience. Consistently engaging in such practice also enhances the functioning capacity of the right brain. The more we exercise this capability, the greater our ability to concentrate.

Using new words or sentences with an unconventional twist can facilitate retaining complex information. For example, to memorize a person's name and date of birth, we can associate an object or event with that person's name. This creates a mental association that allows us to effortlessly recall both details.

> Once, an old man was asked about his date of birth, and he said, "I do not remember, but the day I was born is a day when people distribute sweets made of sesame seeds and jaggery, commonly known as *Tilgul*." This implies that he was born on 14th January, on Makar Sankranti, a popular festival celebrated in India.

Memorizing science or Math formulae can be made easier by integrating them into musical patterns, like a song, tune, or jingle. This approach makes the learning process engaging and helps in better comprehension and long-term retention. A trick to remember a particular route is to associate it with the names of the shops on either side of the road. This can help enhance our focus and memory.

Let's read about Ramesh, who turned his monotonous job into a creative activity, paving the way for greater success.

> Ramesh was a young, exceptionally creative person. He started working at the left-luggage counter in a large mall. People entering the mall would deposit their luggage at the counter and collect a token from Ramesh. After making their purchases, they would show their tokens to collect their baggage. Ramesh managed the storage and retrieval of the bags based on the tokens throughout the day. Soon, the job became tedious and monotonous, as thousands of visitors frequented the mall.
>
> Then, Ramesh thought creatively and adopted a fresh approach, transforming what seemed mundane into an enjoyable experience. He performed the same tasks in a novel and unconventional manner, thus increasing his concentration. Whenever he issued tokens to the visitors, he would keenly observe distinct traits about their hairstyles, eyes, and so on, and mentally link them to the bags and their storage locations. Upon their return, he would effortlessly identify their bags and hand them over without the need to check the token. He took immense pleasure in fulfilling his duties this way.
>
> One day, a businessman visited the store. After shopping, when he returned to collect his bag from the left-luggage counter, Ramesh effortlessly picked up the correct bag without looking

at the token. Surprised by Ramesh's precision, the businessman inquired, "Excuse me, how did you know this is my bag?"

"Sir, you have a unique hairstyle, and that's how I remember you."

The businessman was intrigued by Ramesh's unique talent and offered him a job as a storekeeper at his factory. Ramesh happily accepted this new offer to manage the inventory. He was equally creative in this new venture. He used his creative talent to link the date with incoming and outgoing materials. He knew every detail, from the issue dates to the dispatch schedules. Inventory figures were at his fingertips. He precisely knew when and how long the material would be in the store. With this innovative approach and diligent work ethic, Ramesh quickly became a prized employee in the company.

His distinct skills led him to a well-deserved promotion. Ramesh soon became the personnel manager and was tasked with overseeing the company's hiring procedures. There were around 4000 to 5000 employees in the company. Yet, with his remarkable talent and creativity, Ramesh remembered each employee's name and birthdate. His uniqueness helped streamline his work and infused it with excitement and joy.

We can also employ similar techniques to simplify and infuse curiosity and novelty into our work. This will boost our concentration and help us achieve our goals more quickly.

Use both the left and right brain

If we use only the left or right brain to accomplish any activity, we will eventually experience mental fatigue, hampering our concentration. Hence, we should use a combination of both. For example, if we engage in an analytical activity for a long time, we should switch to a creative activity. We can participate in activities like playing musical instruments or learning a language. We can engage our non-dominant hand in simple tasks like brushing teeth, writing, etc., thereby activating the non-dominant part of the brain and thus balancing it.

3

Compete to Grow, Not to Compare

If a man achieves victory over this body,
who in the world can exercise power over him?
He who rules himself rules over the whole world.

~ Vinoba Bhave

As we explore different ways to make our work more engaging, there is yet another way to breathe new life into what we do. We are all familiar with the concept of "competition." Just hearing the word competition stirs excitement, evoking images of events like the Olympics, Cricket World Cups, or Wimbledon, where athletes and players from around the globe compete for victory and global recognition.

Competition adds a spark to our efforts, boosting our focus and drive. While it is often said that pursuing our passion brings freedom, the key to happiness lies in discovering joy in whatever we do.

> Srikant worked at a nuts and bolts manufacturing company, where the repetitive nature of the job could easily make the work feel monotonous. Those who work in such factories know how quickly the routine can become mechanical—just producing nuts and bolts, day in and day out.

One day, tired of the drudgery, Srikant decided to break the monotony and add a bit of excitement to his day. He turned to his colleague, Ajay, who was working on the adjacent machine, and proposed a friendly challenge: "Hey Ajay, let's have a little competition until lunch. Let's see who can make more nuts."

Ajay initially laughed at the idea, but later found it intriguing and agreed. With a shared sense of camaraderie, both threw themselves into the task, racing to churn out as many nuts as possible before lunch. When it was time to tally their results, Srikant had to face defeat—Ajay scored more.

But Srikant was not discouraged. "Wait until after lunch," he said with a smirk. "I've got a trick up my sleeve."

After the break, they resumed their friendly competition. This time, Srikant's skills shone through, and he emerged victorious in the second round. With newfound enthusiasm and energy, both embraced the challenge. Their spirits lifted by the friendly rivalry!

Soon, Srikant and Ajay began competing every day. One day, the supervisor made an unexpected visit to the factory. He was taken aback by the remarkable speed and efficiency with which Srikant and Ajay were working, especially since the other workers were moving more sluggishly.

Impressed by their exceptional performance, the supervisor approached them. "How are you two managing to work so efficiently? You're both doing an outstanding job!"

With smiles on their faces, they shared their secret. They explained how their friendly competition motivated them to push each other to perform better and added an element of excitement to their otherwise routine tasks.

Upon hearing this, the supervisor's mind began to buzz with ideas. Recognizing the opportunity to boost productivity, he devised a plan. The factory operated in different shifts, and he saw potential in transforming this daily competition into something larger. He gathered all the workers and introduced this new challenge. "Let us hold a friendly competition between shifts," the supervisor announced. "The shift that produces most nuts and bolts will be declared the winner."

The announcement sparked a wave of healthy competition among the employees. With renewed motivation, everyone threw themselves into their work, driven by the prospect of victory. As a result, productivity soared across the factory. At the end of the day, the supervisor proudly displayed the impressive tally of nuts and bolts produced by the first shift on a large board.

When the second shift arrived, they were determined to surpass the first shift's record. With unwavering focus and determination, they worked tirelessly to outdo their counterparts. By the end of their shift, they proudly added their impressive numbers to the board, eager to leave their mark.

The bar was set high, but when the night shift took over, they, too, embraced the challenge with enthusiasm. Working tirelessly under the factory lights, they surpassed all expectations and set a new record, emerging victorious in this spirited competition.

The results were clear: the factory experienced a significant surge in productivity. What started as one employee's simple idea sparked a remarkable turnaround, infusing the entire workplace with renewed energy and excitement.

Healthy competition drives both individuals and organizations to thrive, reaching new heights of success. It eliminates negative emotions such as envy and malice, fostering a positive environment where everyone is motivated to enhance their skills and abilities. They do not seek to belittle others but aim to elevate themselves. The drive to excel and innovate strengthens their concentration and fuels their passion.

This raises an important question: Can we also bring such vibrancy to our work? Can we foster joy and motivation by creating a healthy, competitive environment? Isn't it possible?

The key lies in embracing healthy competition. Whether a student strives for better grades or a business owner aims to increase profits, competition serves as a powerful catalyst for growth. By challenging ourselves alongside peers who excel, we not only learn from each other's strengths but also find the motivation to push our boundaries and step outside our comfort zones.

If we ever find our enthusiasm waning or our focus slipping away, we should not hesitate to seek support from our colleagues. By fostering a healthy, competitive environment, we can reignite our passion for the work at hand.

Healthy, positive competition helps us progress. Healthy competition is focused on improving ourselves and performing better each day. The drive to progress and innovate sharpens concentration and fuels enthusiasm for the task at hand.

However, negative competition proves detrimental to both ourselves and others. Hence, avoid any form of rivalry that leads down the wrong path. Honestly, introspect whether competition breeds ill will, jealousy, or unhealthy comparisons. For example, questioning why someone else got a better job or drives a fancier car is not healthy competition—it is comparison, and it can be counterproductive.

Therefore, weigh the pros and cons before competing with others. If the drawbacks outweigh the benefits, consider competing with yourself instead. When you work independently, you compete with yourself. Reflect on how you can improve your work to achieve better quality in less time. The true challenge lies in surpassing our previous achievements.

For instance, if reading a book feels boring, keep some colored pens and paper nearby. Set specific goals, like "I will read X number of pages today, reflect, and take notes." At the end of the day, assess your progress—note your accomplishments and identify areas for improvement. Adjust your goals for the next day, perhaps by reading a few more pages or revisiting both old and new content.

In this way, engage in daily competition with yourself, gradually increasing both your productivity and enjoyment.

Similarly, reflect on ways to improve your work efficiency each day. Challenge yourself to step out of your comfort zone and push your boundaries. Seek opportunities for healthy competition to make your work more engaging. Ultimately, the power to shape your progress and growth lies in your hands.

As you engage in competition, your concentration will naturally increase, and your intellect will become more receptive, energizing you. When the mind is engaged and revitalized, you will effortlessly focus. It is often said, "True freedom lies in doing what we love, but true joy comes from loving what we do." Hence, embracing healthy competition within your work can serve as an effective way to enhance both engagement and concentration.

4

The "Act As If" Technique

The successful warrior is the average man with laser-like focus.

~ **Bruce Lee**

It is commonly observed that most people begin their work with great enthusiasm, but either leave it midway or gradually try to finish it. The initial interest and enthusiasm with which they start their work wane within a few days. As momentum slows, motivation often dwindles, and the initial excitement gives way to a lack of drive.

Why does this happen? Most of the time, the work is more challenging and time-consuming than expected. Hence, it takes time to see tangible outcomes. During such times, perseverance is needed to pursue it consistently. However, if one faces criticism or a lack of recognition for their efforts, they may feel frustrated and demotivated to continue. They might consider the task a burden rather than a source of accomplishment. The initial excitement stemming from the newness of the task wears off, and the work feels monotonous. One begins to procrastinate on it. Gradually, other priorities take precedence, and this work lags behind.

In other words, when one loses interest in that work, it becomes increasingly challenging to stay focused on accomplishing it. People often express this loss of drive with phrases like, "I'm just not in the mood to do this."

However, it is not always possible to abandon the work that disinterests us and continue with the work that interests us. Sometimes, we must persevere and complete the work no matter how disinteresting and challenging it is.

But how can we reignite this sense of purpose, rekindle our drive, or improve our mood?

Let's explore this with an example.

> You may have heard of Laughter Clubs. Dr. Madan Kataria established the first laughter club in 1955 in Mumbai. Soon, the momentum gained widespread popularity in approximately 100 countries. At their core, these clubs offer a space for individuals to engage in group laughter, harnessing its therapeutic benefits. Initially, they begin by pretending to laugh, whether they feel like it or not. Yet, they simply act as if they are laughing, but soon they start genuinely laughing. The contagious nature of laughter often spreads throughout the group, and even bystanders can't help but join in.

In other words, they bring laughter into action first, and then emotions follow naturally. This approach is known as the "Act as if" technique and is incredibly effective. We need to apply the same technique to enhance concentration.

If you are not in the mood to do a particular task, act as if you are genuinely interested in that task. Tell yourself, "I'm so excited! I'm going to complete this task today," or "Wow, I'm going to learn more about this fascinating topic!"

As you start acting as if you are full of energy and enthusiasm, you signal your brain that you are excited and have begun working on a task. Your brain, in turn, instinctively seeks ways to make the task more engaging. It begins to generate positive feelings about the work at hand. Your mind becomes ready to carry on the task; your feelings eventually catch up with your actions, and your concentration naturally improves.

Usually, our emotions significantly impact and drive our actions. However, in this technique, we reverse that process. Instead of waiting for the right mood or emotions to arise, we act out those actions. As actions and feelings are closely connected, once we begin, our emotions follow suit, aligning with our actions.

Let's use this technique to overcome morning inertia. Despite knowing the benefits of waking up early, getting out of that cozy bed often feels like an overwhelming task. So, to overcome morning sluggishness, use the "Act as if" technique. Act as if you are full of energy. Instead of lying in bed, begin by leaping out of bed as if you are fully energized. Tidy up, brush your teeth briskly, and perform all other morning tasks with speed. As you engage in these actions, you will feel a surge of energy. Tasks that once seemed to take forever now get done in a few minutes. This shift not only revitalizes the mood but also sets you up to seize the day ahead.

This process is similar to the behind-the-scenes work in a movie. When an actor is given an emotional scene, the director often allows them time to immerse themselves in the required mood. The actor acts as if they are truly experiencing those emotions to evoke the right feelings.

For example, in a scene that calls for anger, the actor might raise their voice, throw objects, and contort their face into an angry expression. By intentionally portraying these actions, the emotion of anger gradually surfaces. Once that emotion takes hold, the actor effortlessly performs the scene with authenticity and conviction.

Similarly, when happiness feels out of reach, act as if you are overflowing with joy. Start by laughing out loud, even if it feels forced at first. Before long, you will genuinely begin to feel happier. Get into action, and the emotion will follow naturally. You must practice this unconventional approach to watch the transformation unfold.

Now, you need not wait for the right feeling to arise. Instead, when you are not in the mood to do something, just start acting as if you are keenly interested in it and start working on it. Soon, the feeling will arise. Otherwise, you end up wasting your valuable time waiting for the right mood to strike, leaving you stuck and unproductive.

> Imagine you come home feeling exhausted and hungry, and ask your mother to serve you food. She responds, "I didn't cook today." You are puzzled and ask, "Why not?"
>
> She replies, "I just wasn't in the mood to cook. How can I cook when I don't feel like doing it?" You respond, "Oh, Mom! You can't just say you didn't have the mood to cook!"
>
> Now, imagine if this continues for a few days and she still doesn't feel like cooking, what will happen to you?
>
> In another scenario, your father comes home and says, "I resigned because I wasn't in the mood to work." Just imagine how your household expenses will be managed without his salary.
>
> If your favorite athlete announces, "I am not in the mood to play today; I will play some other time when I feel like playing." Can you imagine the outcome of the match?
>
> If soldiers stationed at the country's border suddenly return home, saying, "We're not in the mood to engage in battle today. We'll stay home and relax." Can you imagine what will happen to the country and your peaceful living?

If everyone keeps waiting for the right mood or feeling to arise to act and doesn't do any tasks until then, can you imagine how life will be?

Therefore, make a firm resolution not to waste time waiting for the right mood. The moment you catch yourself thinking, "I'll work when I am in the right mood because that is when I will be able to focus," Stop. Take a pause! Apply the "Act as if" technique and begin working as though you are already deeply engaged in the task. You will soon notice that your mood shifts, the right feelings emerge, and your focus will naturally follow.

5

Creative Experiments Anyplace Anytime

If you can keep playing tennis when somebody is shooting a gun down the street, that's concentration.

~ Serena Williams

Peter Piper picked a peck of pickled peppers.

She sells seashells on the seashore.

Fred fed Ted bread, and Ted fed Fred bread.

Betty Botter bought some butter, but the butter was bitter, so she bought some better butter to make the bitter butter better.

You must have heard such tongue-twisters during childhood and perhaps tried to say them at some point. Reciting these lines requires a lot of concentration. Every word must be pronounced rapidly with full attention so that the mind doesn't drift, and while reciting them, a sense of playfulness also remains. Interestingly, these playful challenges are excellent tools for improving concentration.

There are many creative techniques that can help boost our focus. You can practice them anytime, anywhere, to enhance your concentration. Let's explore some of them.

1. Tongue twisters

A tongue-twister is a word, phrase, or sentence designed to be difficult to articulate because of a succession of similar consonantal sounds. It is a great way to practice and improve pronunciation and fluency. We must repeat them intensely to avoid errors, thereby improving concentration. If we stumble in between, it turns into entertainment. With repetition, the neural pathways in the brain are reinforced, leading to improved focus.

So here is the trick: practice these tongue twisters at a fast pace to boost concentration. The fun of a tongue twister lies in saying it quickly and continuously.

For example, try saying "Cycle rally - lorry rally - cycle rally - lorry rally," or "Road roller - road roller," or "Good blood - bad blood - good blood - bad blood."

These exercises not only help improve our concentration but also enhance our ability to recall information. They provide a playful and effective way to remember even the most challenging words.

2. Brain gym

Games like Sudoku, Chess, jigsaw puzzles, scrambles, and Solitaire are excellent for refreshing the mind and boosting concentration. These games require significant focus and also enhance decision-making ability.

Just as regular physical exercise strengthens our body's muscles, our brain also needs to be exercised. Mental exercises, such as these games, build mental stamina, enabling us to maintain focus for longer periods.

Find 10 differences.

Most of these games are available online, allowing you to play them anytime, anywhere. However, it is important to stay mindful and avoid overindulging in digital gaming. Make sure to set time limits for these activities. Otherwise, excessive gaming can lead to wasting your valuable time and increasing stress and anxiety, which may harm your mental well-being instead of strengthening it. Remember, these games are meant to relax and rejuvenate the mind, not to stress us out. Keep in mind that moderation is the key to achieving the best results.

3. Connect with Nature

Spending time in nature and engaging in activities like gardening is another effective way to enhance concentration. One feels refreshed and energized when surrounded by nature. The plants and flowers in the garden provide a sense of calm and rejuvenation, helping to sharpen focus.

Every day, we should take time to walk in the garden or simply connect with nature. This can significantly enhance our mental clarity.

According to a 2014 study, planting certain plants in the workplace or at home can boost concentration and productivity, as they purify the air, creating a healthier environment for better focus. This is why plants are often placed in office spaces to enhance air quality and work performance.

Consider adding one or two plants to your home or workspace to cultivate a positive atmosphere. If you are new to gardening, start with easy-to-care-for indoor plants that require minimal maintenance.

4. Exercise

Begin your day with a simple exercise to get your body moving. Research has shown that exercise stimulates the release of dopamine, norepinephrine, and serotonin in the brain. These neurotransmitters play a crucial role in enhancing concentration and regulating mood. Physical exercise helps relax muscles and reduce stress in the body. Since the body and mind are closely connected, when the body feels energized and healthy, the mind becomes calm and content.

In a study conducted in 2018, researchers found that 116 fifth-grade students who exercised regularly for 4 weeks showed improvements in their concentration and attention span.

In another study conducted on older adults, it was revealed that engaging in moderate aerobic exercise or physical activity helped prevent memory loss within just one year.

5. Listening to music

Music has a relaxing effect on the brain. Light or soft music can help boost concentration. Experts agree that classical music and natural sounds, such as the sound of flowing water or birds chirping, effectively enhance focus. Additionally, there are specially curated music tracks and soundscapes to improve concentration and aid mental clarity. Even singing or humming tunes can be beneficial, as these activities help to relax the mind and promote a sense of focus.

6. Balanced nutrition

A balanced diet is essential for optimal focus and mental clarity. This is because the brain relies on healthy fats for proper function, and excellent sources of these beneficial fats include foods like nuts, berries, and coconut oil.

Furthermore, research highlights the significant benefits of incorporating blueberries into our diet. Their unique enzymes can improve concentration and memory for up to 5 hours by enhancing oxygen and blood flow to the brain, thereby also aiding in learning and retention. Similarly, green leafy vegetables such as spinach, rich in potassium, contribute to sharper brain function by accelerating the connections between neurons.

Beyond specific nutrients, maintaining stable blood sugar levels is crucial for sustained brain energy. Choosing a diet rich in fruits, vegetables, and fiber helps regulate blood sugar. Conversely, it is advisable to minimize or avoid sugary foods and beverages, as their tendency to cause rapid fluctuations in blood sugar can lead to feelings of drowsiness and dizziness.

7. Use a timer

A simple yet effective technique to boost concentration and productivity is using a timer or alarm to help the brain focus on a specific task. Choose a task you want to complete, then set a timer or alarm for 20 minutes (or more, depending on your preference). Focus solely on the task until the timer goes off. Once the alarm beeps, take a 5 minute break—get up, stretch, or walk around. After the break, reset the timer and continue working. This method, also called the Pomodoro Technique, is highly effective in enhancing concentration and productivity.

8. Counting words

Select a 7 to 8 line paragraph from a newspaper or magazine and count the number of words in that paragraph. This exercise may seem boring, potentially causing your attention to drift away. Despite the temptation to give up, continue counting until you finish. Recheck to ensure you haven't missed any words. This exercise is quite helpful in minimizing errors while solving multiple-choice questions (MCQs) in competitive exams and also boosts concentration.

Improving concentration is a gradual process that requires consistent effort; it doesn't happen overnight. Professional athletes such as golfers, sprinters, and gymnasts dedicate considerable time to honing their concentration skills. They carefully structure their training regimens to optimize their focus and perform at their best during competitions.

Mastering the ability to focus on what truly matters is essential for success in both professional and personal life. By enhancing your concentration, you can achieve more of what you value and feel better while doing it. This focus is not only important for completing tasks but also for creating time for enjoyment and happiness, allowing you to lead a balanced, joyful, and fulfilling life.

6

Closed Eye Experiments For Enhanced Focus

The strong-minded will not faint,
even when all is lost; the elephant stands firm,
even when wounded by a shower of arrows.

- Thiruvalluvar

Meditation is the best way to channel the mind and enhance its concentration. As one delves into meditation, concentration increases, and with increased concentration, it becomes possible to delve deeper into meditation. In this way, meditation and concentration are intertwined.

While many people struggle to concentrate, this issue is even more pronounced among the youth. Their inability to maintain focus often leaves them feeling restless and frustrated, leading to frequent failures. Meditation is the most effective method for breaking this mental habit and improving focus.

The mind becomes focused in meditation, enabling it to delve deeper into any topic. Even if one desires to achieve success in the external world, a focused mind is essential. A focused mind is necessary for better study. As concentration improves, memory retention enhances, and the mind stops wandering. A focused mind helps pierce through the stream of thoughts, transcending them to attain inner peace and bliss. Indeed, miraculous achievements in this world follow as a result of a focused mind. Hence, meditation plays an important role in enhancing concentration.

While practicing meditation, the mind may grow weary and begin to make excuses, inducing stupor and an urge to quit meditation. However, with patience, the mind gradually becomes more receptive, allowing us to delve deeper into meditation. With regular and consistent practice, the medley of thoughts begins to cease. Both the body and mind begin to feel rejuvenated, increasing our focus. The power of a focused mind is limitless. Such a mind becomes ready to undertake intense work. Therefore, daily meditation practice becomes all the more important.

Methods to enhance concentration

Let's understand some simple experiments with closed eyes that you can practice anytime, anywhere to improve focus.

1. **Reversing the spelling of a name**

   Close your eyes and try silently pronouncing your name in reverse order in your mind. For example, try saying "Anita" as "Atina." Attempt as many names as you can.

   The mind needs to focus while carrying out this exercise, and all other thoughts automatically stop. All scattered thoughts converge and focus on a single task. With regular practice, the mind's concentration power will improve, which will eventually lead you to the depths of contemplation and meditation.

2. **Practicing mental math**

   In this experiment, practice mental mathematical calculations as outlined below.

   - Close your eyes and try to recall some random numbers. Now start multiplying them in your mind and try to remember the answers.

- Since this exercise requires mental calculations, refrain from using any calculating devices, tricks, or rapid calculation techniques.
- For example, consider the numbers 47 and 22. Close your eyes and try to multiply them mentally.
- Once you have the answer, open your eyes. Then verify your answer by multiplying these numbers on paper.
- It is advisable to begin with simple numbers like 22 to simplify the mental calculation until you become more adept. You can consider more complex numbers later, such as 47 × 28. Practice multiplying various combinations of numbers daily to enhance your concentration skills.

While practicing mental Math, you may notice that you can maintain your grip on those numbers for a while, but then you lose track of them and try to hold onto them again. Throughout this process, your concentration improves over time.

3. **Listening to music in meditation**

Listen to some serene music, such as gentle flute music. You can easily find it online. Listen to the track carefully for a while and then turn the player off. Now sit in a meditative posture, close your eyes, and try to recall the sound of the flute. Although the music is no longer playing outside, you will hear it from within. Focus solely on the flute music and ignore any other sounds.

During this meditation, make it a practice to join the tip of your thumb and index finger on each of your hands. This gesture, also called a *mudra*, serves as an anchor to train the mind. With consistent practice, this mudra becomes a cue for the mind, indicating that it is time to focus. The mind recognizes the cue and settles into meditation more easily. Although you can use any pair of fingers, it is essential to consistently use the same pair for the mudra to be effective.

This anchor button serves as a valuable tool, especially during stressful situations, offering a means to de-stress. With consistent practice, the anchor will become more effective.

During this experiment, you may find that your mind easily recalls the flute music at some times, while at other times, it may falter. This happens because the flute music is not being played outside, but you are recalling it in your mind. If you are familiar with it, you will find it easier to recall. Otherwise, you will struggle to recall it.

Practice listening to different sounds each time you meditate, alternating between various instruments. This diverse approach will enhance your concentration. Furthermore, this technique not only improves concentration but also helps sharpen your memory.

Practicing these different mental exercises strengthens mental resilience, enhances concentration, and fosters a sense of peace. Moreover, the mind is trained to remain in the present rather than constantly oscillating between the past and the future, leading to relaxation and tranquility. Having learned the art of being focused, the mind no longer wanders or engages in incessant thinking, allowing it to function at its best and maximizing productivity.

7

Set at Least One Goal

People with goals succeed because they know where they are going. It's that simple.

~ Earl Nightingale

Another secret to improve concentration is having a goal that occupies your mind day and night, provides direction to your life, and changes its condition.

Contemplate: Have you set a grand goal for your life? If not, have you set even a small goal for the coming year regarding what you will accomplish? Have you planned a roadmap to elevate yourself to the next level of growth? Or do you believe you can manage life without any goals?

> Two friends were sitting together, reminiscing about their past. One of them said, "Can you believe it's already been 5 years? It's astonishing how quickly time has flown by, achieving one target after another, and pursuing our life goals! It feels like just a few days ago we were in college, lazing around, chitchatting."
>
> The other friend spoke in a subdued voice, "Yes, only 5 years have passed, but it seems like an era has passed. My life feels monotonous. I feel stuck in the mundane pursuits of daily life,

switching between home and office. I am at a crossroads, unsure of the direction I am heading."

Have you noticed that the first friend was full of excitement and zest for life, while the other seemed completely dejected and listless, as if he were not living his life but merely carrying the burden of existence?

What could be the reason? Both were of the same age; yet for one, life was as light as flowers, while for the other, it was a burden like a mountain.

The answer is clear. The first friend navigated life with a definite goal. He had big dreams he wanted to achieve, and as a result, his life was filled with excitement and contentment. In contrast, the other friend lacked a goal. He didn't know what he wanted to achieve or in which direction to guide his life.

Those with a goal can visualize their destination clearly and are fully energized and motivated to achieve it. Their goal not only transforms their future but also their present, making them automatically more focused on achieving it.

If your goal is to become a great athlete or sports person, you need to go to the field and practice the sport regularly. However, if your goal is to become a doctor or engineer, you will have to sit down and study. In other words, both your present and future will change based on the goals you set and the actions you take. Moreover, your ability to concentrate improves when you set a clear goal and work toward achieving it.

Often, we are unaware of a goal, and even when we are, it may not be powerful enough to motivate us to pursue it. In such situations, it becomes challenging for our body, mind, and intellect to focus on the goal due to a lack of passion to achieve it.

For instance, an obese person who enjoys eating may set a goal to lose weight but struggle to focus on it and pursue it, as they will need to adhere to a diet that restricts their eating preferences. Therefore, setting a goal and having a strong desire to achieve it is the most essential step in increasing concentration.

Whether the goal relates to any area of your life—be it passing a competitive exam or striving to lose weight—the more intense your desire to achieve the goal, the more focused your mind becomes on accomplishing it. Therefore, setting a specific goal and committing to it is essential for success, regardless of how small or large the goal may be.

Once you set a goal, you become fully aware and determined to achieve it. At times, you may not achieve the desired result, yet remain steadfast in pursuing your goal, just like an ant. An ant trying to climb a wall slips down multiple times but continues to climb with the same enthusiasm and energy. Similarly, while working toward your goal, if you encounter failure, learn from it, get up, make progress, and persevere on your journey until you reach your destination.

You can also set reminders that help you stay on track. Let's understand how reminders helped achieve goals using some examples from Indian history.

- After his insult by the Nanda king, Dhanananda, in Pataliputra, Chanakya, the famous Indian polymath, vowed not to tie his tuft of hair until he exacted his revenge by uprooting the Nanda dynasty and making Chandragupta Maurya the king. His open tuft of hair constantly reminded him of his goal. Once his vow was fulfilled, he finally tied his hair, signifying the completion of his mission.
- In another example from the Indian epic Mahabharata, when Draupadi was humiliated in the royal court, she took a solemn pledge that she would not tie her hair until it had been washed with the blood of the very hands that had dared to touch her. This was a public declaration of her resolve for revenge and a constant reminder of the injustice she had suffered.

You don't need to go to such extremes to create reminders. However, these examples can help you understand the importance of creating reminders, a practice that has been prevalent since ancient times, to stay focused on one's goals.

If you are preparing for an exam, you can pledge not to indulge in watching TV or engaging in social media until your exam is over. Alternatively, resolve to stay away from gadgets altogether. If your goal is to save a specific amount every month, you can set reminders to help you maintain discipline. You might reduce eating at high–end hotels and limit shopping sprees to essentials only until you achieve your savings goal. This way, you can align your reminders with your goal.

Every night before going to bed, ask yourself, "What have I done today that will take me one step closer to my goal/s?" If the answer is "nothing," then get up and complete a small task that aligns with your goal, no matter how insignificant it might seem.

In a survey, people were asked about their goals. Their responses led to 4 distinct categories. The first category stated, "Yes, we have a goal, but it's in our minds." The second group said, "We have written down our goals." This category performed slightly better than the first. A third category mentioned, "We have written our goals and read them every morning when we wake up." The fourth category expressed, "We ask ourselves every day what we have done today to achieve the goal."

Which of these categories do you belong to? Have you set a clear goal? How often do you remember it? Did you write your goal down in a diary and forget about it, or do you read it every day? Are you making any effort to achieve it?

Connect with your goal as if you have married it, so that it becomes your motivation, waking you up in the morning and compelling you to act. Just as in a marriage, if someone does not wake up on time, their spouse might nudge them, "Hey, how long will you sleep? Get up now. Don't you have to go to work?" Similarly, if you marry your goal, it will wake you up: "Come on, get up now and work; you have a big goal to achieve."

However, if you wake up in the morning and think, "Oh no! It's Monday again. What am I going to do? I just can't concentrate on my work," then ask yourself, "What is my goal?" If you don't have a goal, define a goal for yourself. The least you can do is have a goal to improve your concentration. That can also be a significant step toward self-development.

8

Channelize Your Energy

Concentrate all your thoughts upon the work at hand,
The sun's rays do not burn until brought to a focus.

-Alexander Graham Bell

There was a young man who couldn't swim. Whenever he saw his friends swimming in the river, he would think, "I wish! I could swim too." He longed to experience the thrill of diving into the water from high up, just like his friends did. The idea of swimming across the river excited him.

One day, he ventured to the river alone. There was no one else on the bank. He mustered some courage and tried to step into the water. He was hesitant but cautiously waded in. However, the moment his foot touched the water, a sudden, sharp fear gripped him. He panicked and hurriedly fled back home.

A few days passed by, mustering his resolve, the youth once again returned to the shore. This time again, the pattern repeated. He would put one foot in the water only to nervously back away. However, he began frequenting the river. He gradually started venturing further in, repeating his attempts and inching forward a little more each time.

A little further downstream, a fisherman who cast his net every day happened to witness the young man's attempts. He couldn't help but laugh heartily at the young man's determined yet fruitless efforts.

One day, the fisherman saw the youth approaching the shore. He brought his boat to the riverbank, called the youth closer, and inquired about him. While conversing with him, the fisherman made him sit in his boat and headed toward the middle of the river. As they sailed, the fisherman began talking about swimming. The youth listened to him while thoroughly enjoying his ride on the water.

When the boat reached the middle of the river, the fisherman suddenly pushed the youth into the water. The youth was startled, and his heart pounded with fear. He didn't know what to do for a few moments. He then regained his senses and frantically tried to get back to the boat, moving his hands and legs in a desperate attempt.

But as he got closer to the boat, the fisherman pushed him back into the water. He kept trying to reach the boat, but the fisherman prevented him every time he was about to touch it. Eventually, the young man understood the fisherman's motive, and his fear gradually began to subside. Now, he started enjoying this game.

After a couple of rounds, the fisherman pulled him into the boat. As he sat, grooming his wet hair, he asked, "Uncle, what time should I come tomorrow to learn my next lesson?"

The fisherman laughed aloud. "Son," he said, "You have already learned the biggest lesson today that no one learns swimming by standing on the shore. You need to muster the courage to get into the water to swim. It is said that once you're thrown into the water, you'll instinctively learn to swim, but for that, you must focus all your energy on swimming. Your hands and feet, mind and intellect, passion, senses, and awareness need to be channeled in the same direction. If you can do this, you can emerge from any storm safely. The key is to channel your energy in one direction."

The youth learned his lesson thoroughly to channel his energy in a single direction. It not only helped him in swimming but also in all aspects of life. Our energy is also often scattered in different directions. We must gather it and focus on our goal.

Many times, people set out with a clear goal in life. However, their energy gets divided among various daily activities. Consequently, they cannot fully concentrate on their goal and continually postpone their efforts toward it. This lack of focus often leads to consistent failures, despite their initial intentions.

Let's understand this with another example.

> A 12th-grade student preparing for his board exams set a goal to prepare for the CA entrance test along with the 12th-grade exam, intending to pass both with good marks. However, he was often distracted. Sometimes, he would receive calls from friends and spend hours talking to them. Other times, someone would invite him to watch a movie, and he would spend an entire day out. Occasionally, he would spend his day playing games on his phone. When it was time to study, he would think, "Oh, I feel so exhausted today. Let me sleep now. I will surely study harder tomorrow." With all these distractions and diluted focus, an entire year passed, and he could not pass the CA entrance exam.

Similarly, most people often fritter away their energy without focus, or they have become accustomed to multitasking, which inevitably divides their focus and energy. For example, when they are at home, they simultaneously eat food, watch TV or a web series, talk to their children, and keep an eye on their phone notifications. They also engage in many activities simultaneously at the office, such as screening multiple files on the laptop, talking on the phone, delivering a presentation, and preparing for another important meeting.

This behavior is not limited to a few individuals but affects everyone, regardless of age. Even a little child learns it by observing their elders. In this way, many people squander their time on trivial pursuits. When it's time to focus on important activities aligned with their goal, they feel completely exhausted and eventually postpone working on them.

If the student in the above example had refrained from talking on the phone for long or aimlessly roaming around and had saved his time and energy, channeling it in the right direction, he would have achieved his goal.

Energy has immense power. It can perform tasks such as cooking, lighting a fire using paper, matches, or a stove. It can also cause explosions and generate electricity.

When energy is gathered, its power increases manifold. For example, rain falling from the sky may not wreak much havoc because it is essentially nothing but scattered water droplets. However, when these droplets are collected in one place, they fill huge dams. If this accumulated water breaks open the dam, it can cause a catastrophe, destroying everything in its path. The scattered raindrops lack such power, but that power multiplies when it accumulates in one place. This is the power of accumulation.

Have you ever focused the sun's rays on a piece of paper or the tip of a matchstick with a magnifying glass? The paper or matchstick catches fire in a short time. If you remove the magnifying glass, the sun's rays alone cannot burn the paper or the matchstick directly because the rays are scattered all around. Only by directing the energy of those rays through the magnifying glass can fire be ignited.

Likewise, you need to gather all your energy, sharpen it like a laser, and direct it toward attaining your goal. This will help you stay focused on a single task.

Contemplate and list all the activities that drain your energy in various directions. For example:

- How much time and energy do you spend talking or playing games on your phone or other electronic gadgets?
- Do you engage in multiple tasks simultaneously that dilute your energy?
- How much time and energy do you spend idly watching TV, movies, and web series?
- How much energy do you waste on unnecessary trips to the market, excessive cleaning, and so on?

By contemplating this way, you will realize why your energy is scattered. Once the causes are identified, you can take corrective action. Only then can you reclaim the diverted energy, directing it toward tasks that align with your goal, and work on your goal with full concentration. When all your energy is channeled in a single direction, any goal, no matter how challenging it may seem, can be accomplished easily.

9

Work with a Timetable

A person who is gifted sees the essential point and leaves the rest as surplus.

~ Thomas Carlyle

We have recognized the importance of having a clear goal, as it enhances our concentration. However, can we achieve it simply by writing it down on paper? No, we need a roadmap and a timetable to accomplish it.

Having a roadmap involves planning for the goal by creating a timetable and thoroughly considering all aspects of the goal, as well as potential problems, in advance. While we often create plans, we neglect to set a timetable that specifies which tasks to execute when, making it difficult to achieve the desired results.

Let's understand the importance of a roadmap and timetable with a story.

> Once, a person was driving his jeep through a forest. He wanted to reach a temple on the other end of the forest.
>
> On his way, he spotted a cute little rabbit. He was so fascinated by the rabbit that he got out of the jeep and began chasing it. While running, he noticed a beautiful deer. Forgetting about

the rabbit, he started to follow the deer. In this manner, he kept chasing one animal after another. By the time he realized it, it was already dark, making it difficult for him to navigate out of the forest.

The same thing happened the next day. In this way, many days passed, and gradually he forgot about his original purpose of visiting the temple outside the forest. He became engrossed in the mesmerizing flora and fauna of the forest.

Here, rabbits and deer symbolize the enticements we encounter in life that distract us from our goals. By the time we realize this, we have already wasted away our precious time.

One of the most common rabbits that entices us is social media, which consumes our daylight. We often lose track of the time spent on such frivolous activities. OTT platforms have only added more spice. Once lured into this virtual web, we feel trapped. These habits eventually lead to addiction and devour a lot of our energy and time. Such distractions have significantly weakened our ability to concentrate.

Another common sight is when people get sidetracked at work by an email that grabs their attention, a WhatsApp notification that just beeped, or a call from an acquaintance. Sometimes they become so engrossed in these distractions that they forget how much productive time they have wasted on them.

If we want to progress toward our goal, we need to safeguard ourselves from these modern-day rabbits and deer. To achieve this, we must create a roadmap and timetable that will remind us of our goals and keep us on track.

For instance, if the person had decided on a time to reach the temple or simply thought about getting there before dark, he would have been more mindful of the time spent chasing the rabbit and would have achieved his purpose of going to the temple.

Contemplate whether you have a clear plan and timetable to achieve your goals.

For instance, if you have set a goal to score above 90% in the exam, you need to create a timetable accordingly. If you aim to score 60%, you still need a plan and a timetable to achieve that goal. Even if you want to achieve 50% or even fail, your timetable should reflect that, ensuring you don't mistakenly pass. In other words, create a timetable based on your goal, and you will stay focused while working according to that timetable.

Creating a timetable essentially involves dividing your time into smaller, more manageable segments to complete your work in a planned and organized manner.

> Dr. Pavlov, a Russian physiologist and psychologist, once conducted a small experiment on his dog. Every day, when it was time to feed his dog, he would first ring a bell. He did this regularly. Eventually, as soon as the bell rang, the dog would suddenly become happy and start jumping excitedly.
>
> Once, Dr. Pavlov rang the bell, even though it was not the dog's feeding time. When the dog heard the bell, it began salivating and became excitedly agitated, jumping around. Observing this, Dr. Pavlov concluded that when a task is performed in the same manner at the same time for an extended period, the body becomes accustomed to it and develops a habit.

For instance, some people habitually meditate first thing in the morning. Regardless of where they are—at home, in a hotel, or while traveling—their bodies are naturally conditioned to meditate each morning. They wake up at their scheduled time and get ready to meditate. This highlights the importance of having a timetable.

However, despite creating a timetable, unexpected events can occur, such as surprise guests, urgent tasks, or longer-than-anticipated calls, causing us to deviate from our planned timetable. In such situations, our timetables or plans may sometimes fail.

Let's consider some important points before creating a timetable to address these eventualities.

1. To begin with, you can use your phone calendar to create your own timetable. It is quite easy and convenient. You can write all your activities in sequence in it.

2. The next step is to ensure your timetable is flexible. The timetable should not be too tight, with back-to-back tasks and no breaks. For instance, 8:00 – 9:00 AM for task A, 9:00 – 10:00 AM for task B, 10:00 – 11:00 AM for task C, etc.

   If your timetable is too tight, adhering to it will be a challenge. Incorporate breathing spaces between tasks. For example, if task A is scheduled from 8:00 am to 9:00 am, either scope it in such a way that you complete it in 45 to 50 minutes, or schedule task B for 9:10 am. During these short breaks, you can make a quick phone call or engage in stretching exercises that help build physical mobility. It is best to relax before fatigue sets in, and then proceed with the next task. Be sure to take breaks for 5 to 10 minutes and avoid distractions during that time.

   If you wish to use a timetable at your office where you work for eight hours at a stretch, plan short breaks of 4 to 5 minutes after every hour. Use this time to stand up and stretch, relax both mentally and physically, or handle minor tasks if you are experiencing fatigue or stiffness from prolonged sitting. This approach helps you avoid interruptions during your work and manage any emergencies effectively.

3. When preparing a timetable, it is essential to know when your energy levels are high and low. Some people have high energy in the morning, while others have it at night. The quality of work during high-energy periods tends to be better, and more work gets done in less time. Concentration levels also peak during these times. Therefore, tackle tasks

that are difficult and require greater concentration during high-energy periods.

Usually, we tend to work on tasks that are easy or interesting during our high-energy periods. For instance, students often tend to study their favorite subjects when their energy is high; however, this is not the right approach. We can complete our interesting tasks regardless; high energy is not needed for that. More energy is required for tasks that either seem challenging or that we dislike. Therefore, work on your favorite tasks when your energy is low and tackle difficult tasks when your energy is high.

Experiment with this for a week to determine its effectiveness and how well you can adhere to it—70%, 80%, or even more. Revise the timetable as necessary and then gradually prepare a final timetable based on your observations. If you need to complete an important task or project by a specific deadline, create a special timetable for that. For example, students should create a special timetable for exams. If you are working on a major office project, create a special timetable for it.

When you resolve to complete a goal within a fixed time, it becomes a dual goal. This dual goal significantly boosts your energy and helps you focus. By implementing all these strategies, you will be better able to achieve your goal.

10

Inculcate the Habit of Asking Questions

If you focus on results, you will never change.
If you focus on change, you will get results.

~Jack Dixon

Pre-schoolers are inherently curious. Known to be bright-eyed and bushy-tailed, they bombard their elders with endless questions, yearning to explore the world. Due to their innocence and limited understanding, elders often struggle to provide them with the appropriate answers. As a result, their inquisitiveness is often met with dismissive silence or hurried, half-hearted answers. Repeatedly receiving unsatisfactory answers stifles their curiosity. The spark of curiosity, once so vibrant, begins to dwindle, replaced by a cautious reserve. As they grow, they become less likely to ask questions and more focused on giving answers.

Schools fare no better. Children are not allowed to ask too many questions. As a result, they only specialize in writing and rote learning answers, rather than asking questions. Moreover, they become so accustomed to this that questions stop arising within them. They begin to agree with and accept everything without thoroughly understanding it. When the teacher asks the class, "Did everyone understand?" they agree with everyone else, even if they haven't understood it.

This childhood habit persists into adulthood, leading to a tendency for passive agreement on everything. When assigned a task by their manager at work, they instinctively agree, only to regret later, "Oh, I don't know what the boss expects from me. I already told him, 'Yes.'"

They feel intimidated when asking questions, whether in meetings, in the classroom, or to strangers. They do not express their opinions or thoughts and tend to keep things to themselves. As a result, they often either don't fully understand the situation or misinterpret what has been said.

It is crucial to ask questions without hesitation and seek clarification when necessary. Asking the right question at the right time and in the right manner is indeed an art.

Imagine, in the middle of the historic battle of the Mahabharata, if questions had not arisen in the mind of the Pandava prince Arjuna and if he had not asked those questions to Lord Krishna, would we have the Bhagavad Gita today? It was Arjuna's very questions that led to the Bhagavad Gita, a compilation of questions and answers between Arjuna and Lord Krishna.

We also need to redevelop the art of asking questions and seeking answers to gain clarity, thereby avoiding misinterpretations and misunderstandings.

Often, asking questions is perceived as a sign of weakness. Those who avoid asking questions think, "If we ask something, people might consider us stupid and assume that we don't understand even simple things." However, after asking questions, we become more aware and alert. We feel that since we have asked a question, we need to pay relatively more attention to the answer.

In fact, if we have a question related to our goal and the necessary concentration required to attain it, we should seize the opportunity to ask questions without hesitation. By internalizing this art of asking questions and seeking answers, we demonstrate our curiosity, attentiveness, and commitment to learning. Never shy away from asking questions, no matter how simple they may seem. Questions help accelerate our understanding of the given topic, making us more aware. When we ask questions, we are not just seeking information; we are actively listening and learning. Hence, cultivate curiosity, ask more questions, and become more aware and mindful.

But to whom should we ask the questions? Whenever we determine a goal, we must first question ourselves, "Why have I chosen this goal? What am I going to gain from it?"

Secondly, we can ask questions to someone we trust to guide us correctly and who has accurate information about our interests and goals.

Further, what kind of questions should we ask? Before asking any questions, we should consider these six fundamental questions: What, Why, Where, When, Who, and How. They need not follow a specific order; the latter questions may be asked first.

Let's understand how Rajiv achieved his target by asking questions.

> Rajiv worked at a paint company that wanted to expand its business. Therefore, they opened a new unit to increase production and entrusted all responsibility for that unit to Rajiv. Initially, this unit produced small batches of paint. Rajiv faced the challenge of increasing the volume of paint production with the existing workforce. This was a substantial target to meet.
>
> Rajiv rolled up his sleeves and got to work. He started gathering as much information as possible from his branch manager and began brainstorming and asking questions to himself. Questions swirled in his mind, "What strategies can we implement to double the volume of paint? What workforce adjustments will be needed? What will be the staffing levels for each shift, and what will their working hours be? What will be the required volume of raw material? How many packaging boxes will be needed? Where and how will the finished products be stored?"

While doing this, he also sought guidance from his seniors and outlined a clear plan with specific timelines on paper. With this strategic and meticulous planning, he started taking baby steps with full concentration. He started by procuring raw materials and securing a space to store them. He motivated the workers and encouraged them to work in different shifts, producing more by working overtime with an incentive. He worked with relentless focus. He reviewed and refined his plans from time to time by asking relevant questions and ultimately achieved his goal ahead of schedule.

From this example, we understand two aspects:

1. **Working with a goal:** A well-defined goal serves as a catalyst for productivity and achievement. With a goal in sight, we are mentally and physically prepared to work toward it. We become more focused and energized.

2. **Asking questions to achieve goals:** Questions illuminate the path, guiding us toward our destination. By asking questions, we create a clear roadmap that makes it easier for us to reach the destination. Questions help in achieving challenging goals.

Questions do not always have to pertain to our goals; they can also be about achieving anything we desire in life.

Once, two friends were strolling down the street. They saw an elephant with a mahout sitting on it, approaching them. Seeing this, the first friend said, "Let's ask the mahout to give us his elephant." The other friend replied, "Are you crazy? Why would he give his elephant to us?"

The first friend replied, "Yeah. But there's no harm in asking. What's the worst that could happen? He may refuse. If he disagrees, it's okay, but if he agrees, we'll get an elephant!"

Never hesitate or fear asking questions. If you do not get anything, so be it, but if you do, you might even get an elephant.

Many people do not get promoted because they never ask for it. Similarly, when people go on a shopping spree and see the *fixed rates* board on the store wall, they refrain from bargaining. They do not even ask for a discount. However, if they push past their hesitation and inquire, they might receive a discount. There is no harm in asking.

Often, people get out of a cab and begin frantically searching through their pockets for a small amount of change, such as 5 rupees, instead of simply asking the cab driver, "Hey, would it be okay if I don't have the exact fare? I am short of 5 rupees right now?" The driver might just say, "Sure, that's fine. You can give it to me next time we meet."

Some people refrain from asking questions because their ego gets in the way. They often think, "Why should I ask? Others should ask me." Avoid making such mistakes; by not asking questions, you incur a loss.

There is another dimension to asking questions. Before asking questions, take time to contemplate the topic thoroughly. "Have I really not understood the topic? Is it right for me to ask this question? Will this time, this place, and this method be right?" After considering numerous aspects of the topic, the mind naturally begins to focus. Consequently, we find answers to some of the questions from within, which helps to open our intellect.

Therefore, we must never hesitate to ask questions. Unless we ask questions, our goal won't become clear to us. As soon as a question arises in our mind, we naturally become aware of seeking its answer, fully concentrate our mind to find that answer, gather our energy at one point, and start advancing toward our goal. While making strides to achieve our goal, sometimes our questions may change based on circumstances and time, and so do their answers. Hence, it is essential to periodically review our work by asking questions.

11

Focus on What You Want

The true art of memory is the art of attention.

~ **Samuel Johnson**

In November 1890, Swami Vivekananda stayed in Meerut to rest and recover his health. He loved reading books by different authors. He was a voracious reader from childhood and enjoyed reading spiritual and philosophical texts. One of his disciples, Akhandanandji, would bring him books from the local library.

One day, Swamiji expressed his desire to read some books written by Sir John Lubbock, a renowned thinker and philosopher. Akhandanandji brought a collection of books from the local library, which Swamiji remarkably finished reading within just one day. The next day, the books were returned to the library.

This continued for several days, during which Akhandanandji would pick up a huge pile of books from the library and return them the very next day. The librarian was surprised to see this.

When Akhandanandji returned to the library to pick up some more books for Swamiji, the librarian asked him, "Sir, do you actually read the books you borrow? It seems like you just flip through the pages and return them. I have to search for different books for you every day."

Akhandanandji told Swamiji about this conversation. The next day, Swamiji went to meet the librarian. Politely, he said to the librarian, "Akhandanandji comes here daily to bring me books. I read all of them in a day and returned them the next day. Are you doubtful that I returned them without reading?"

The librarian said, "How can anyone read the books of a profound philosopher like Sir John Lubbock in just one day? I find it hard to believe."

Swamiji replied, "I understand your concern. However, I have read all the books attentively in one day. If you still doubt me, you may ask me any question from any of these books we borrowed."

Despite Swamiji's assurance, the librarian could not believe his words. Therefore, he asked Swamiji a few questions about Sir John Lubbock's work. Swamiji not only answered these questions but also provided the page numbers where the answers could be found in the book. The librarian was utterly flabbergasted. He was amazed by Swamiji's extraordinary memory and brilliance. He bowed and apologized to Swamiji, "I'm curious to know how you manage to read so many books in a single day and then remember what you have read?"

To this, Swamiji replied, "Oh, that's quite simple. To remember what you've read, all you need is concentration. If you read a book with full concentration and undivided attention, remembering it becomes easy."

When you accomplish any work with concentration, its impact becomes apparent in your life. This applies not only to reading but also to other areas of life. When you focus on something with concentration, it leads to your growth, and that thing either begins to materialize or multiply in your life.

In a study conducted on plants, it was observed that plants that received more attention developed better than those that received less attention. Similarly, when you pay attention to children, they become brighter, healthier, and more capable, and develop good qualities.

To summarize, whatever you focus on begins to manifest and grow in your life. If you consistently think about your goals and the things you wish to achieve, these very thoughts will attract and manifest them into your reality. For example, if you aspire to become a successful businessman, you will find yourself doing those things that will turn your vision into reality. The more you direct your focus toward your goals and desires, the quicker they will materialize in your life, provided you make a firm resolve, keep your words and actions aligned with your goal, and maintain your focus on them.

However, if you even mistakenly focus on your fears or what you don't want, those fears will intensify and cloud your judgment. This can lead you to engage in wrong actions, steering you away from your intended goals.

To become the kind of person you aspire to be or to achieve a certain level of financial success, it is essential to maintain a consistent focus on your goals. From dawn till dusk, your actions should align with and propel you toward your goals.

This does not mean that you should avoid other tasks or conversations with people if they arise while working toward your goal. The key is to maintain your focus on your goal, even while participating in these activities.

Contemplate: What are you currently focusing on in life? Do these things help you achieve your goals? Have you defined a clear goal for your life?

Focus on what you truly want. If your goal is to improve your health, pay attention to it, and you will see it improving. If you desire more loving and caring relationships, begin nurturing them; your relationships will become stronger and more fulfilling. As you focus on developing yourself, your life will undergo transformation.

12

Tratak Meditation

Put all your eggs in one basket – and watch that basket!

-Andrew Carnegie

Let's explore *Tratak* meditation, also known as Yogic Gazing, to increase concentration. It holds great significance in the practice of yoga. Those who practice yoga and meditation are likely familiar with this technique. It is an effective tool to help anchor the mind during meditation. It is not only a method to calm the mind but also an excellent way to achieve mastery in concentration.

Among the five senses of the human body—the eyes, ears, skin, tongue, and nose—the most information reaches the brain through the eyes. To taste or feel something, we must physically taste or touch it. In contrast, the eyes can observe and gather information from objects that are miles away.

In Tratak meditation, both the eyes and the brain concentrate on a single, preselected point. Consequently, distracting thoughts are eliminated, and the mind becomes calm.

Following are the steps to practice Tratak meditation:

1. Place a picture of a horizon at a distance in front of you, with a burning candle placed before it.
2. Keep the candle at arm's length so that its flame aligns with your eyes, neither too high nor too low, to prevent any strain on your eyes and ensure comfort.
3. If you wear glasses, choose a comfortable distance for placing the picture and the candle, as this exercise should be done without glasses.
4. Now sit in a comfortable posture. Slowly move your eyes from left to right and then from right to left. Then slowly move them from top to bottom and vice versa. After this, gently rotate them clockwise, and then anti-clockwise. Once your eyes are relaxed, proceed with the meditation.
5. Now, stay still and gaze at the candle flame without blinking for a minute and a half.
6. If you cannot gaze for that long at first, begin with a few seconds and gradually extend the time.
7. Ensure you do not blink during this time. Even if you blink, do not consider it a failure; it is a natural and common occurrence at the beginning.
8. Continue practicing even if you blink.
9. Sit comfortably and continue gazing at the flame calmly without straining your eyes.
10. Now close your eyes and visualize the picture in your mind's eye. After observing the picture for a while, it will naturally appear on your mental screen.
11. As the mental image gradually fades, open your eyes and gaze at the flame again for a few seconds or as long as you can, without blinking. Then close your eyes and visualize the image again.

12. Continue this practice of seeing the picture outside and visualizing it inside. Through practice, you will understand how long it takes to form a clear mental image.
13. Gradually increase the duration of each session and continue with your meditation practice.

When you practice this meditation for the first time, it is normal to blink your eyes a few times. Gradually increase the meditation duration; do not rush and take care of your eyes. Increasing the meditation time not only strengthens the eye muscles but also improves concentration and helps eliminate distracting thoughts.

Continue to gaze at the flame of the candle until the mental image of the picture is formed. Science states that if you observe any picture for 14 seconds, its mental image begins to appear on your mental screen with your eyes closed. If you still cannot see the image, keep observing the picture with open eyes for a little longer. As the mental image begins to emerge, try to hold it on your mental screen for as long as possible.

In this meditation, you get to see the games that the mind plays. When we intend to gaze, the mind repeatedly urges us to blink. Although it is a spontaneous action that does not require effort, the mind insists on blinking the eyes even more when you focus on meditating. In such moments, remind yourself, "It's okay; I will continue looking at the picture." Just sit comfortably and continue gazing without straining your eyes. You can blink your eyes after the stipulated time is over.

Sometimes you may feel bored during this meditation, and your mind might question, "How long do I have to sit here? Do I just keep gazing?" Doing nothing can be challenging for the mind. However, you have to encourage yourself to stay seated. When the mind feels bored sitting idle, it will turn its attention toward the flame. Then, slowly increase the duration of your practice. Consistent practice of this meditation trains the mind, eyes, and brain to improve concentration.

13

Backtrack Your Thoughts

Only when your consciousness is totally focused on the moment you are in, can you receive whatever gift, lesson, or delight that moment has to offer.

~ Barbara de Angelis

You must have experienced that the speed of the mind is faster than even the wind. One visual or incident is enough to trigger a flurry of thoughts. The mind is not bound by time. One moment it is captivated by the scene before us, and the next moment it reaches out to a relative living in another country or a far-off city. At one moment, it dwells in the present, and the very next moment, it is swayed by memories of the past. And before we know it, it is already busy planning for the future.

The mind's speed is such that almost 50,000 to 60,000 thoughts pass by in a single day. Yet, despite these countless thoughts, how much do we really accomplish in a day? Hardly 15 to 20 tasks! Shouldn't we then be getting only thoughts meant to execute those tasks? But the nature of the human mind is such that it keeps producing an endless stream of idle, wasteful thoughts. The restlessness of the mind greatly hinders our concentration.

But what is this mind? In reality, the mind doesn't have a physical existence. We can easily pinpoint where our ears or nose are on the body. We also know where the liver or heart is located inside the body, but can we locate the mind? No!

Isn't it ironic that we spend our entire lives fulfilling the desires of our mind, yet we don't even know where it resides within us? This is because the mind is not a physical organ, but rather a bundle of thoughts.

Just as the constant circulation of blood indicates that the body is alive, the continuous stream of thoughts in the mind is an inherent characteristic of the brain that regulates the body's functions. As a result, various thoughts flow through the mind throughout the day. These distracting thoughts prevent us from maintaining focus.

The mind is akin to a child who, while playing with one toy, upon seeing another, abandons the one in hand and chases after the new one. While the mind is focusing on one topic, another thought suddenly occurs, and we start thinking about it, without realizing when and how this shift happened.

To enhance concentration, the mind needs to be trained to focus on a single topic for a long time. For that, it is essential to regulate its speed and cultivate the habit of being in the present.

When we wake up in the morning, the first thought that arises is, "I woke up." Then, gradually, the flow of thoughts begins to increase. "What tasks are to be accomplished today? Oh, am I late? Is the tea ready? What's for lunch? I need to meet this client today… and so on." An endless chain of thoughts begins.

And if something unusual has happened, those thoughts also begin to surface. In case of an argument, fight, disagreement, or some disappointing news received, the same thoughts keep running in the mind throughout the day, with no sign of stopping. Consequently, we struggle to focus on the task at hand as the mind does not receive the space it needs to concentrate.

When the mind is caught in a whirlwind of thoughts, we lose track of what we are doing. We often get sidetracked while we think.

At times, we might enter a room wondering why we are there in the first place. This occurs because of the rapid speed and traffic of thoughts racing through the mind.

In the outside world, a vehicle slows down in traffic congestion, but the opposite is true for the mind. The faster the mind races, the more congested it becomes with thoughts.

The mind, by its very nature, struggles to concentrate fully amidst a torrent of thoughts. Each time we begin working on something, the mind tends to drift to other thoughts, leaving us lost in a state of disorientation for hours. When we realize this and resume the task, we get lost in the web once again. Thus, the mind struggles to achieve 100% concentration on any task at once, leading to frequent pauses in work.

Let's understand this with an example. Someone was focusing on a task, but their attention was divided between the task at hand and daydreaming about their plans. As a result, they could concentrate only 50% on their current task. They had to allocate more time for the remaining 50% of the task. However, as they resumed their work, the same issue occurred, and they could focus only on 50% of that 50% task, which was 25% of the original task. The remaining 25% was still unfinished. Due to the mind's tendency to focus only 50% on the task at hand, each time they attempted, they could only complete 50% of the task. Consequently, they had to revisit the same task repeatedly.

To escape this mental congestion, we need to train the mind to be fully present in the present moment. While it may seem difficult at first, with a little effort, the help of some techniques, and a bit of willpower, it will be possible.

Thought-reversing technique

Whenever we try to focus on a task and a distracting thought enters the mind, we can use this technique to keep the mind grounded in the present moment and regain our focus.

As we know, during traffic congestion, some people reverse their cars to get out of it. Similarly, whenever our mind is caught up in thoughts and our focus drifts, we should consciously observe and reflect on how the current thought arose. What were we thinking before that? We should then delve deeper to identify the underlying thought or emotion driving it. In this way, we should keep tracing back through each thought, and eventually try to reach that initial thought from where our focus drifted. With this technique, we will be able to return to our work, exactly where we left off.

Let's understand this with an example.

> Suppose you are working on a project on your laptop. Suddenly, you realize that instead of focusing on the project, you are thinking about something completely different and unrelated. At that moment, you have to seize your thoughts and become fully aware of them.
>
> For instance, you discover that your mind has stopped focusing on the project and has drifted to thoughts about your foreign tour or a vacation. Now, trace the thought back. Ask yourself, "What triggered the thought of this foreign trip?" Try to find its preceding thought. The thought of a foreign tour came from family, and the thought of the family came from wanting to impress relatives, and the thought of relatives came from how people flaunt their status at the office. The thought of the office folks came from the canteen thought - the canteen thought came from the best sandwich there - the thought of sandwich came from a party - the thought of a party came from the idea of a promotion - the thought of a promotion came from wanting to build a better project. And this led you back to your project, and your eyes landed on the project program running on your laptop. With this, you return to the present moment. This is the Thought-reversing technique.

By tracing back your thoughts, try to identify the specific thought that caused your mind to wander. Initially, you may find it challenging to practice. You might only trace back a couple of thoughts at first.

However, with consistent practice, you will become more skilled at delving deeper into your thoughts. Soon enough, you will be able to concentrate fully, giving your 100% to the task at hand. Your mind will gradually learn to remain in the present moment. Simultaneously, the distractions caused by racing thoughts will diminish, helping you gain control over the restlessness of your mind and enhance your concentration.

14

Selective Attention

To do two things at once is to do neither.

~ Publilius Syrus

Once, a Guru and a disciple were strolling through the woods, engaged in deep conversation. The disciple seemed a bit worried. He asked the Guru, "How can some people face any situation calmly while others get agitated even with minor incidents? As soon as an incident occurs, their mind is flooded with all sorts of thoughts of everything that happened before and after. They always seem troubled by the past, even in the present."

The Guru replied, "To remain calm in any situation, we must remember three words – Awareness, Detachment, and Concentration. Let's understand them with the help of a story."

> In a jungle, an elephant was happily and peacefully feeding on the leaves of a tree, when a bee started buzzing around its ear. The elephant tried to shoo it away by shaking its head while continuing to eat the leaves. When this repeated several times, the elephant asked the bee, "Hey, why are you buzzing around so troubled and making noise?"

The bee said, "I just can't focus my attention on one thing. My mind gets attracted to almost everything around me, and I get stuck in it. But you don't seem to be distracted at all. I have been buzzing around your ear, but you don't seem troubled at all. Instead, you're happily enjoying your food."

The elephant replied, "Yeah! I'm enjoying my food because I'm not paying attention to anything else. I solely focus on one thing at a time. When I'm eating, I pay full attention to it, so I savor every bite. I am fully detached from whatever else is happening around me. I have total control over my mind and senses. I'm neither affected by external distractions nor drawn by stray thoughts. I focus on one task at a time."

On hearing this, the disciple's face lit up. He exclaimed, "That is so true, Master! If we do not pay much attention to the distractions around us and remain fully detached while doing our work, we can focus on our work completely."

To summarize, to achieve our goal, we must be mindful of distractions around us while staying focused on a single task. With this, all our energy will be invested and channeled into one task, and the quality of our work will also improve.

What is selective attention?

At any given moment, we are bombarded with a constant stream of sensory information. However, we don't pay attention to each one of them; instead, we focus our attention on certain essential elements and ignore the rest. This is selective attention. It acts as a cognitive filter, helping us prioritize and direct our attention toward the most relevant things while ignoring distractions.

Attention is a limited resource. The ability to selectively focus our attention plays a vital role in our daily lives. It helps us focus on a particular object in the environment for a specific period. It enables us to focus on essential tasks, make informed decisions, and process information efficiently. It allows us to filter out unimportant details and concentrate on what truly matters.

It is exceptionally effective when it comes to focusing fully on a topic or task and setting aside all distractions for a specific time. When we switch from one task to another, the mind is generally not ready to make that switch. Instead, it remains stuck with thoughts and memories of the previous task. Consequently, it becomes challenging to detach or disengage from the last task. With selective attention, we can deliberately detach from the prior task and focus on the current task fully.

Let's understand this with a few examples.

1. A lawyer mulled over his court cases even after returning home. He was so absorbed in his upcoming case that he couldn't switch off from legal matters even at home. His wife and kids felt distressed. They wanted to talk and spend quality time with him, but he was so preoccupied with his own thoughts that he was emotionally unavailable to his family. Hence, it was crucial to disconnect and detach from his previous task; only then could he concentrate fully on the current task.

2. Umesh was a student. He needed to complete his school project. While working on the project, he received a message from his friend Jayesh, asking for help in solving a problem. Despite being in the middle of his project, Umesh left it midway to help Jayesh. However, while he was solving the problem, thoughts about completing his own project kept drawing his attention. As a result, his focus became divided. He could neither effectively solve Jayesh's problem nor make any meaningful progress on his own project. To make matters worse, he was unsure which task to prioritize. He was caught in a dilemma.

In such situations, begin by making a conscious decision to finish one task completely. Either complete your project or help your friend solve their problem. When you decide to take up one task at a time and focus on the other task later, you temporarily set aside thoughts related to the other task and complete the prior task in the least possible time without unnecessary distractions.

3. Ajay, a software professional, was engrossed in developing a software program when his manager unexpectedly called him to a meeting. Although he didn't want to leave work midway, he also needed to attend the meeting. In this situation, if he could detach himself from the programming task and approach the meeting with a fresh mindset, he would participate more effectively in the discussion and recall it better. But if his mind was preoccupied with thoughts of the software program, he would neither benefit from the meeting nor do justice to the program code. So, he felt at a loss on both fronts. He wasted his time and drained his energy, leaving him feeling frustrated. Had he practiced selective attention, focusing on one task at a time, he could have dedicated himself equally to both tasks and completed them more easily and efficiently.

Selective attention does not imply ignoring a task or conversation completely. It means giving undivided attention to whatever work you are doing at the moment. When you switch from one task to another, you prevent yourself from getting stuck in a stream of thoughts about the previous task.

Concentration and selective attention should be practiced together. Selective attention can be improved with practice and daily effort. Beginning with small tasks and consistent practice, it can boost your productivity.

15

Maintain Proper Body Posture

With concentration, success is assured.

~ Anonymous

We have all heard that clothes reveal one's outward personality. However, to know their inner thoughts and feelings, we need to understand their body language and physical gestures. A person's body posture reveals much about them when speaking to someone, explaining something, or trying to grasp a concept. It demonstrates how attentively they listen, their level of comprehension, and their emotional responses to what they hear, whether they are bored or captivated. Their gestures and expressions convey everything, without the need for words. In today's terms, we refer to it as their body language. We can gauge a person's state of mind by simply observing their body language.

There is a deep connection between the mind and the body posture. For instance, you may have observed how people adopt a relaxed or casual posture when conversing with their family, friends, peers, or those of similar age. They often seem indifferent and exert minimal effort in listening or fully comprehending what is being communicated, nor do the words profoundly impact them.

However, when the same people talk to their superiors, respected individuals, or their boss, they straighten up, become more alert, and listen attentively.

Similarly, a person's posture can greatly reflect their commitment to work, their ability to concentrate, and the level of self-control they possess over their thoughts and emotions. Therefore, if you genuinely want to engage in any task or delve deep into a subject, you must be aware of your body posture.

In our childhood, we were often advised not to study while lying down or sitting on the bed, as it would make it harder for us to retain what we learned. We were encouraged to study either by sitting at a table and chair or on a mat laid out on the floor. This approach helped us stay more attentive. The likelihood of feeling sleepy or dozing off while studying reduced significantly. Moreover, it was easier to take notes while sitting. This posture allowed us to maintain an appropriate distance between our eyes and the book, which safeguarded our eyesight and helped us focus better on our studies.

In today's context, what posture should we adopt to enhance our concentration? Things haven't changed much because we are still the same as we were in childhood. To stay focused, we should maintain a comfortable posture to avoid distractions so that our attention does not drift too often.

Sitting for a longer duration often causes discomfort in our body that disrupts our ability to concentrate. Hence, to stay focused, it is important to find our body's center of balance. We need to learn to keep our spine aligned, enabling us to sit and work comfortably for longer durations.

Center balancing technique

Following are the steps to achieve center balancing:

1. Sit on the chair with your back straight, leaning slightly forward.
2. Gently tighten your knees and release them.
3. Keep your feet together.
4. Slowly lean your body back a bit, then return to the center and pause for a moment. Now, move a little forward, and pause again at the center. Lean back slightly again and pause in the center. In this way, gently sway your body back and forth, pausing briefly at the still point.
5. Keeping your spine straight, repeat this exercise 4 to 5 times.
6. Settle at a point in the center where it feels comfortable to keep the body straight and naturally aligned.
7. After you have balanced the forward and backward movements, repeat the movement sideways. Like a pendulum swinging from left to right, pausing at the center of the arc, lean to the left first, then return to the center and pause. Now, move to the right. Gently pause at the center again.
8. Keep your back straight and feel the stretch on your sides. Repeat this exercise 4 to 5 times.
9. In this process, too, pause at the center and find a point where it feels naturally balanced to hold your body.
10. This center point is the ideal alignment for sitting. Aligning the body with this center balancing method minimizes fatigue and discomfort while sitting, allowing us to sit comfortably for extended periods.

The center balancing technique allows us to stay focused and work for longer durations. Essentially, it balances the gravitational force acting on the body.

Therefore, avoid doing any important task while sitting on the bed or sofa because the cushions are soft. When you sit on them, your posture may not align with the gravitational force, which can cause discomfort in your body. This can lead to pain and fatigue over time, prompting you to prop them up.

Hence, while you sit, make sure you are fully supported by the chair, with your feet flat on the floor and your body relaxed. Ensure your posture is comfortable, as excessive stiffness can make it difficult to stay focused. With this relaxed posture, you will be able to concentrate easily. Always remember the secret, "Still body, still mind." In other words, a calm, still, and stable body leads to a focused and attentive mind.

16

Maintain the Right Mindset at Work

Concentration purifies and calms the surging emotions, strengthens the current of thought, and clarifies the ideas.

~ **Swami Shivanand**

Emperor Akbar, commonly known as Akbar the Great, was the third Mughal emperor who reigned in India from 1556 to 1605. Once, while hunting, he wandered deep into the woods. It was evening and time for his prayer. Facing the west, he prepared to offer *Namaz* (prayer) when a woman suddenly ran past him. Her husband had not yet returned home, so she was frantically searching for him. In her haste, she passed by Akbar, and her foot accidentally brushed against his. He became furious, but as he was busy praying, he couldn't express his anger. After a while, he finished his prayer and stood up. Just then, he saw the woman approaching with her husband.

"How dare you?" Akbar asked sternly. "You kicked me, and that too when I was praying!" The woman pleaded, "I am so sorry; I was so frantically searching for my husband that I didn't realize when I brushed against you. No other thought crossed my mind at that time except for finding him."

She continued, "He was just my ordinary lover, my worldly husband, yet I completely lost my composure. But you were praying to the Almighty God of Love. Your attention should have been completely on Him alone. How did you even realize my foot brushed against you?"

It was then that Emperor Akbar realized for the first time how prayer should be offered. Reflecting on the experience, he wrote in his memoirs titled *The Akbar Nama*, "That tribal woman taught me the secret of where and how our mind should be when we pray."

Prayers offered with a focused mind yield powerful results and are more likely to be answered quickly. True concentration involves being fully present in the present moment, which means being mindful of the present moment.

Imagine mechanically performing the rituals of worship in a temple while your mind is preoccupied with thoughts about business, job, finances, or family. Then the act of worship becomes devoid of spirit and sentiment, much like a stone offering milk to another stone.

If you start working on something and your mind drifts elsewhere, it becomes challenging to focus on that work. Yet, this is precisely what happens when we begin our work. The restless mind often gets lost in past stories or daydreams of the future, forsaking the present moment. However, true concentration can only happen in the present. For that, we ought to have the correct body posture, along with the mind anchored in the present. Until we are both physically and mentally focused and engaged, there is little chance of achieving excellent results.

Following suggestions can help you stay focused in the present moment:

1. Build confidence

Tell the mind, "No matter how boring this task may seem, I must concentrate on it for some time. I can certainly do this at least once, even if it is just for a little while. What is so difficult about it that I cannot do it? I can definitely do it, and it is well within my capabilities." This self-encouragement will reduce mental resistance toward that task and help the mind concentrate.

Despite your resolve, the mind may still resist by thinking, "How much longer? I'll not stick with this for long; it's so boring. There's no fun doing this. It seems too difficult, and so on." However, reaffirm your resolve and get started. As you begin working on it, the mind intervenes intermittently and tries to distract you. But when you ignore it and persevere, it eventually begins to cooperate and focus.

The mind is like a small child who cries to get your full attention and continues crying while looking at you for a while. However, when the child sees that you are not paying attention, they quietly start playing. Similarly, when ignored, the mind quietly works on every task, no matter how boring or challenging it may seem. The mind may perceive the work as boring, but when you complete even the most tedious tasks, it boosts your self-confidence, empowering you to tackle all your responsibilities with full confidence. In this way, by encouraging your mind or ignoring it, you will start focusing on the intricacies of the task, which will help your intellect concentrate on it.

2. Understanding

Given the incredible speed of the mind, it possesses an immense capacity to accomplish a multitude of tasks. Therefore, keep your mind busy by providing it with plenty of work. However, while focusing on one task, the mind tends to wander in different directions. Hence, try to engage your intellect in it.

For example, while listening to a lecture, your mind can wander. Then, tell yourself, "I will not just listen to the lecture, but will also strive to understand it well."

This approach of committing to truly understanding the subject while listening will engage both the mind and the intellect. In this effort, you will mentally process and reiterate what is being heard.

This will prevent your mind from wandering and enhance your concentration.

3. Memorizing

As part of this suggestion, affirm to yourself, "I will not only listen and understand the lecture but will also memorize it well because I am listening to it for the last time. I don't want to listen to it again." If you are listening to it for the last time, how would your concentration be?

Remember your school or college days. As you were heading into the examination hall, your friend suddenly pulled you aside and said, "Hey! I caught a glimpse of the question paper in the teacher's hand. And guess what, I managed to see one of the questions written on it." Hearing this, you immediately grabbed a book from somewhere and started reading the answer. While reading, your concentration was so intense that you were completely oblivious to the crowd of other students pushing their way into the hall. Your concentration remained undeterred.

Then, you closed the book and entered the examination hall. As soon as you received the question paper and read the question, without wasting a single minute, you wrote down the answer to that question, confidently securing your marks for it. What do you think was your last thought while reading the answer? "This is my last chance. I am not going to get to read this answer again." At that moment, your concentration was at its peak. You read, understood, and remembered the answer as if you were reading it for the last time. Then, you recalled and wrote it down immediately.

4. Learning

As part of this suggestion, affirm to yourself, "I will thoroughly understand and learn everything that is being taught in the lecture. If any member is absent, I will teach them the lecture. Hence, I will study diligently to prepare myself in a way that allows me to thoroughly understand, absorb, and then teach it effectively."

This approach makes you reflect on the ways to explain things in a simpler way. Your intellect automatically begins to delve deeper into the topic, which further aids in achieving concentration.

5. Teaching

As part of this suggestion, affirm to yourself, "I will teach others in a way that they can also teach someone else." This means you need to explain the topic thoroughly so that the other person grasps it deeply. The simpler you explain, the easier it is to understand. If you understand it well, you will be able to explain it to others in various ways, using simple language and relatable examples tailored to their understanding. You should not explain it merely by repeating the exact words you have heard in rote language. The only prerequisite is that you must understand it thoroughly. When you simplify it for others, they too will be able to explain and teach it to someone else, passing on the knowledge to others.

Overall, all the suggestions can be summarized as: "No matter how boring the task or topic is, I will listen. I can listen to it at least once. I will listen as if I am listening to it for the last time. I will not only listen but also understand. I will not only understand but remember it. I will not only remember and retain it, but also prepare myself in such a way that I can teach others. I will teach them in such a manner that they too can teach others."

By following these suggestions, you can enhance your mental concentration, which will not only help you but also others.

17

The Art of Listening

He who does not have a concentrated mind,
cannot understand anything, even if he listens.

~ From Narad Purana

Sachin worked in a grain warehouse, where his job involved lifting grain sacks and arranging them neatly. Although he worked diligently, a part of his attention was always on his wristwatch. The watch was a cherished gift and a final memento from his father. Naturally, Sachin valued it deeply. One day, the watch suddenly went missing. Despite searching extensively, he couldn't find it.

Some children were playing near the warehouse. Sachin asked them about his watch, but none of them were aware of it. He wanted his cherished watch at any cost. Therefore, he pleaded with them to find it and even promised a generous reward in return.

The children searched every corner of the warehouse, but to no avail. Sachin's heart sank, and he felt his hope fading. The children returned to play, but Sachin, consumed by grief, sat near the warehouse. His shoulders slumped, and tears silently rolled down his cheeks.

Just when hope seemed lost, a child suddenly emerged from the warehouse, tightly clutching the missing watch in his hand. Sachin was overjoyed to see the watch, but he wondered how this child had found it when he and others couldn't.

He curiously asked the child, "How and where did you find it?" The child innocently replied, "Uncle, I stayed behind in the warehouse when everyone left. When everything was hushed, I heard a subtle ticking sound. It was barely audible, but I stood there silently, figuring out where the sound came from. The faint ticking of the watch led me to a corner, where I found the watch."

Sachin expressed his gratitude and praised the child for his sharp focus. Staying true to his promise, he also rewarded all the children.

The same thing happens to us as well. When overwhelmed with seemingly unsolvable problems, no matter how hard we search, the solution remains elusive. Our mind becomes unstable, hindering concentration. To navigate such situations, we need to calm the mind and achieve stability. Only then can the mind and intellect focus on finding solutions efficiently and effectively.

If you want to determine the direction of your life and steer it accordingly, first work on focusing your mind and sharpening your ability to concentrate. Set aside some time to calm and concentrate your mind amid the hustle and bustle of life. With a focused mind, you can discover ways to solve many difficulties in life.

Cultivating the ability to listen attentively is one of the most effective ways to enhance concentration. It engages our auditory senses as well as brain. Moreover, when we listen to a story with full attention, we start to visualize its scenes in our imagination. This means that, with attentive listening, our eyes also begin to focus on it.

However, according to a survey conducted by researchers, we don't pay full attention to conversations and absorb only a minuscule portion of what is being said. Consequently, we often miss important information.

> Once during a training session, the participants were posed a question: "There were two buildings in a city facing each other. One was a home to honest and good people, while the other housed criminals and bad people. One day, both buildings caught fire. When the ambulance arrived, which building's fire would it extinguish first? The building that housed criminals or the one with honest people?"
>
> Most participants impulsively replied, "The fire in the building with good people should be extinguished first." However, they overlooked a critical detail: the trainer mentioned *an ambulance*, not a fire brigade. An ambulance cannot extinguish a fire; that is the duty of a fire brigade. This highlights the necessity of attentive listening.

Contemplate: How are your listening skills? Do you truly listen, or do you merely hear? If you do listen, how attentively do you listen? Our listening skill can bring our speed of mind under control.

Let us understand this with another example.

> If you are asked, "Out of three items, if you take two, what's left with you?" your immediate response might be "One." However, that's not right. Think again. The answer is actually two. Read it carefully: "Out of three items, if you take two, <u>what's left with you</u>?" The answer is two, as you now hold the two items you have taken. Thinking in terms of subtraction might mislead you into saying "One." But it's not so. This illustrates how we perceive and interpret what we hear.

Listening: The white magic

The fact that we have two ears and only one mouth suggests that we should listen more and speak less. Furthermore, we should listen as if we are listening for the first time. It is possible that we already know what the other person is saying, and the mind may resist listening. However, we should listen to it attentively and treat it as an opportunity to increase our concentration.

Often, when we hear something we already know, we interrupt others halfway through a conversation and say, "Yeah, I know it." Often, when someone else is speaking, we are too busy forming and rehearsing our response in our mind, which prevents us from listening attentively. Therefore, if you are listening to something you have already heard before, observe the other person's expressions and gestures to see if they are explaining it in a new way this time.

Pure listening means listening without any judgment, explanation, or justification. This will develop gradually with regular practice, but it will surely improve your listening ability.

Following are the stages of active listening:

1. **Attentive listening:** Listen to the other person attentively.
2. **Paraphrasing:** Once they have finished, restate what you have understood in your own words.
3. **Empathizing:** Acknowledge and validate their feelings or perspective. This does not mean that you agree with them, but rather that you empathize with them. This way, the other person feels that you have truly heard them, not just intellectually but also emotionally.

Let's understand this with a few examples.

1. Arun told his neighbor Vijay, "You know what happened today? My laptop suddenly crashed." Vijay responded, "Oh no! How did you manage then?" Arun replied, "Well, I went to my next-door neighbor and asked if they had a spare laptop. I even promised to return it later. But nowadays, no one wants to help!"

   When Arun was candidly sharing his struggle, Vijay wondered, "Is he indirectly taunting me?" And that's where the issue began. Instead of attentively listening, Vijay became judgmental.

2. Ravi returned home after a long day at work, and his wife, Reema, told him, "The babysitter took a day off without informing. And then milk was over, and the groceries in the

pantry were running low, so I had to go to the neighbor for help. And this wasn't enough, the dishes were overflowing, and so was the laundry. I work so hard all day, and you..."

Even before Reema could finish talking, Ravi interrupted, "Hey, don't worry, I'll pick up some extra milk and groceries tomorrow. Then you won't need to take help from the neighbor. As for the babysitter, we'll find a reliable babysitter next time. And you don't need to do the laundry all at once."

As soon as Reema heard this, she got angry and said, "Hey! You are not listening to me." In this situation, Ravi didn't realize that he needed to listen to Reema fully and with complete attention before suggesting solutions.

3. Let's consider the same scenario with Neil and Leena. Neil returned home from work, and his wife Leena told him, "The babysitter took a day off without informing, the groceries were running low, the laundry piled up, the dishes were overflowing, and you..." Hearing this, Neil said, "Oh, it sounds like you've had a really tough day today. I can't imagine how much work you had to do. I'm so sorry you had to take care of everything alone. You must be so tired."

   This was pure listening, where Neil neither offered a solution to Leena nor justified anything. He listened to her attentively, restated what she shared, and empathized with her.

Whenever you find yourself in such situations, instead of offering solutions, explanations, or unsolicited advice, listen to the other person. Moreover, don't just listen to their words; try to understand their underlying emotions. Only when you truly and genuinely grasp their feelings will it be complete and attentive listening.

This skill of attentive listening is the white magic of relationships. To master this, you need to practice it daily. Listen to the other person as if you are hearing them for the first time. This will slow down your mind's speed, bring it under control, and enhance your concentration by diving deeper.

18

Stay Away From Gadgets

The power of concentration is a catalyst for success in human life, for it rallies all the other powers of human life to bring about a transformation.

~ Anonymous

It was a usual morning, and the alarm went off. Uma was just about to hit snooze when she realized it was already 8:00 am. She woke up with a jolt, "Oh no! It's already eight o'clock. I better get up; else, I will be late for the 9:00 am meeting. And if I don't show up, the boss will have another chance to yell at me. 'Even if you work late, you must log in by 9:00 am.' Oh, this life sucks."

Muttering to herself, Uma dragged herself out of bed. Grabbing her mobile phone, she headed straight to the kitchen to make some tea. She scrolled through messages on various social media apps. While sipping her tea, her wandering gaze suddenly stopped at the vacation pictures posted by her friend Kamla. Enthralled in the maze of the digital world, she completely lost track of time. It was almost 8:45 am; alarmed by the time, she quickly got up to get ready for the meeting. This was not just a one-day affair but a daily routine for her.

This is not just Uma's story; it is most of ours. Today, in almost every household, people start their day with their mobile phones. Gadgets have become a part of their lives, from the moment they wake up in the morning until they go to bed at night. They are constantly distracted by the beeps of notifications on their mobile phones. If their eyes are glued to the mobile screens most of the time, how can they perform any task with full concentration?

In the olden days, when there were no electronic gadgets, people focused more on their work and were more productive. They would perform one task at a time, ensuring it was completed on time with high quality. However, with time, so many electronic gadgets have become widely available. Their excessive use is negatively affecting people's concentration and productivity. In this situation, most people agree that it is better to reduce the use of these gadgets to maintain concentration.

Here are some practical tips to help you stay away from these gadgets for some time.

1. **Overcome the allure of gadgets:** To perform important tasks, projects, or studies, find a quiet place with minimal distractions, such as a library or a place with weak network coverage, to ensure you can fully focus on your work. Keep a gap of a few hours to check and respond to messages on your mobile phone, and keep your mobile phone away during that time. For instance, instead of frequently checking your messages, set a timer to check them once every three hours. This will enable you to focus completely on your work during that period.

2. **Set screen time for social media and other apps:** Nowadays, most mobile phones are equipped with apps to help you manage your screen time. You can set reminders and monitor your screen time using them. These apps further help in analyzing the time spent each day, providing insights into our digital habits.

For instance, if you spend 5 to 7 hours on your phone throughout the day and then almost the entire next day scrolling through it, that app would let you know exactly how long you were on screen. Once you become more aware of this habit and the time involved, reflect on whether you spent that time without doing any work, and whether it was worth wasting that much time. The insight gained from this reflection will help you regain control of your digital habits, gradually reducing your excessive attachment to gadgets. As you become more mindful of your time and efforts, you will become more focused and productive.

3. **Prioritize focus over money:** If you are using an app that keeps showing ads, either stop using it immediately or buy the premium version. Constant ads drain your focus and emotional energy, leaving your brain too fatigued to concentrate when it matters.

4. **Minimize distractions:** When commercials frequently interrupt your TV viewing, mute the TV. If you can't mute it or if you are in a cinema hall, look away from the screen. When using a mobile phone, flip it down during ads and disable notifications. No notification is worth interrupting your current task. This discipline trains your mind to not get distracted even slightly without your command.

5. **Drawing and coloring:** Neuropsychologist Dr. Stan Rodski states, "Drawing pictures and coloring them elicits a relaxing mindset, similar to what you would achieve through meditation. Like meditation, coloring allows us to switch off our brain from other thoughts and focus on the moment. Tasks with predictable results, such as coloring or knitting, can often be calming. Coloring not only relaxes and calms adults, it also improves concentration in both children and adults."

   In addition, the participants in his experiments experienced a slowing of their heart rates, and their brain waves transitioned to an alpha state, demonstrating that coloring provided the same calming benefits to them as meditation.

According to Dr. Rodski, coloring, painting, or other creative art forms help slow down the flow of thoughts. Eventually, a point is reached where thoughts cease to come. Just 5 minutes of coloring each day is enough to get the same benefit to the brain as about an hour of meditation.

You can also benefit from colors in this way. Whenever you feel the urge to scroll on your mobile, consciously divert your attention by engaging yourself for 5 minutes in drawing or coloring. This will help you focus entirely on the present moment. You don't need to spend much money to practice this. You just need a set of colorful pencils and 10 to 15 minutes of your time daily to draw pictures and color them.

6. **Avoid multitasking:** Multitasking or doing multiple tasks simultaneously might make us feel smart and efficient, but it is actually counterproductive. It weakens our ability to concentrate. Instead, as far as possible, try to focus on one task at a time. You can use the auto-lock system on your mobile phone for this. With this, you can restrict access to specific apps for a pre-defined duration. For instance, during office hours or when handling critical tasks, you can temporarily disable the apps that constantly pull your attention. You can even set this lock for a fixed time each day, ensuring these apps automatically turn off for a few hours, making it easier for you to stay focused.

Gadgets can be both a boon and a bane. They are powerful tools that can either uplift or hinder our growth. Just as a positive mindset can elevate us to great success, a negative one can derail us. Gadgets are not only detrimental but also contribute to wasting our time and disrupting our concentration. However, when used wisely, we can leverage their benefits to enhance productivity, quality of work, and creativity, paving the way for our success. It is up to us to decide whether to use them as allies or adversaries on our journey.

19

Calm the Body and the Mind

The greatest of all dharmas is the godliness of choice and the concentration of the senses.

~ Adi Shankaracharya

When we engage in work that demands sustained mental effort over a prolonged period, we inevitably begin to feel mentally exhausted. While physical fatigue can be alleviated with some stretching or light exercise, mental fatigue can be overcome by simply closing our eyes for some time, offering a sense of calm and relaxation. Interestingly, when this relaxation technique is combined with meditation, it significantly enhances our ability to concentrate.

Meditation is a kind of short nap that allows the mind and body to relax and recharge. Such meditation brings our body, mind, and brain into a state of complete calm and stability, allowing us to concentrate fully on our work again.

Studies reveal that sleep or rest revitalizes our brain, allowing it to function far more efficiently. An average person engaged in moderate physical work usually finds that 7 to 8 hours of sleep in a 24-hour cycle is sufficient. Excessive sleep can negatively impact our ability to concentrate.

This implies that we should take short, restful breaks or practice 10 to 15 minutes of meditation while working or studying, as both can have a similar rejuvenating effect on our mind and body. This practice helps revitalize our brain and increases concentration.

The mindful practice of meditation can strengthen mental fitness and improve focus. It is a time-tested technique to enhance concentration.

You can practice any of the following meditations during short breaks at work or while studying to relax the mind.

Relaxation meditation

1. Sit comfortably and close your eyes
2. Take a few deep breaths.
3. Now picture yourself sitting or lying on a soft lawn in a hilly place, nestled by nature.
4. Feel the serene atmosphere enveloping you.
5. The cheerful chirping of the birds adds to your joy.
6. Immerse yourself in the soothing sound of the gentle ripple of a stream flowing nearby.
7. The cool breeze gently touching your body is rejuvenating you.
8. Feel fully relaxed while unwinding in this serene environment, far from the hustle and bustle of the world.
9. Be in this calm state for 10 minutes.
10. Gently open your eyes and return to the present moment.

Reverse counting meditation

1. Sit in a comfortable place with your eyes closed.
2. Imagine yourself gently descending from the 100th floor of a towering building in an elevator.
3. Your gaze is fixed on the number panel in the elevator. As the elevator descends, the numbers are running in reverse: 99, 98, 97, 96, and so on.
4. As the elevator descends, your mind is also drifting into a deep state, going deeper and deeper, until you enter a serene state of complete relaxation.
5. Soak in this relaxed state for a few minutes, allowing your body, mind, and brain to unwind and feel completely calm. Relax... Relax... Relax...
6. Continue to feel this state for 10 to 15 minutes.
7. Gently open your eyes and return to the present moment.

Feel free to experiment with other techniques during this meditation. For instance, you can visualize counting numbers in reverse order on a blackboard or a whiteboard, or mentally solve a Math equation, like addition, subtraction, or multiplication, as per your preference. These meditative exercises will soothe your mind, leaving you in a state of deep relaxation.

20

Concentration to Know Your True Self

The one excellent thing that can be learned from a lion is that whatever a man intends doing should be done by him with a whole-hearted and strenuous effort.

- Chanakya

Saint Eknath was a revered Indian saint who lived from 1533 to 1599. His spiritual guru, Janardan Swami, was courageous, resolute, disciplined, and a luminous soul. Janardan Swami served the royal court of the King of Daulatabad, balancing his duties of imparting knowledge to his disciples with his own spiritual practice. He was highly respected throughout the kingdom for his proficiency at work. He was a devotee of Guru Dattatreya Maharaj, a revered sage and Hindu deity, often considered an incarnation of the divine trinity of Brahma, Vishnu, and Mahesh.

Janardan Swami's mornings were dedicated to the service of Guru Dattatreya. In the afternoons, he attended to the proceedings of the royal court, and his evenings and nights were immersed in studying the *Dnyaneshwari* and *Amritanubhav*—spiritual texts written by Saint Dnyaneshwar. This was his steadfast daily routine.

During that era, disciples had to rise before the first rays of dawn, even before their guru, and sleep only after their guru had retired for the night. Daytime offered no respite; they barely had time to breathe. Dedicated disciples were so engrossed in their duties that they had no time left for anything else throughout the day.

Eknath, as a disciple, ardently prayed, "Grant me such strength to serve my guru that I alone can finish all the work that ten devotees would together do." He selflessly tended to his guru's needs and stayed vigilant to ensure that his guru's sleep was not disturbed even slightly.

For him, the guru's happiness was his contentment, the guru's words were like divine scriptures, the guru's image was the embodiment of God, and the guru's home was his heaven. Moreover, he served his guru with unwavering devotion, embodying the spirit, "The guru is verily the Supreme Brahman, i.e., My Master is my God."

Once, the guru assigned an accounting task to Eknath. Eknath tried to reconcile the accounts but found one paisa unaccounted for. The guru was sound asleep, but Eknath stayed up all night solving the mystery of the unaccounted paisa. Not for a single moment did he allow himself the luxury of thinking, "It is just about one paisa; I can spot the discrepancy tomorrow." This demonstrates his devotion and dedication to his duties. He always ensured that he finished his work on the same day.

Contrary to this, in today's world, most people have mastered the art of procrastination. They often don't know what they should postpone and what they shouldn't. Ideally, they should delay the urge to indulge their negative tendencies and habits, but they tend to do the opposite. Instead, they postpone acts of service and positive endeavors. They also delay cultivating the essential virtues necessary for fulfilling their duties and responsibilities.

Later in the story, Eknath continued reconciling the account for the missing paisa. The hour was late; the third quarter of the night had already passed. It was almost dawn. Janardan Swami suddenly woke up and saw the glow of a candle. He noticed Eknath was busy with the calculations. All at once, Eknath found the account of that missing paisa and clapped with joy.

Seeing this, the guru approached Eknath and asked, "What happened, Eka?" Eknath beamed and replied, "I found the missing paisa. I am so happy." After hearing his entire story, the guru smiled and said, "You are so happy after finding the mistake of a single paisa. Imagine how happy you'll feel when you realize the mistake you made while creating the world." Through this profound remark, Janardan Swami wanted to convey, "Just think of the profound bliss and celebration that will follow when you become aware of the mistake you made the moment you stepped into this world."

Which mistake was Janardan Swami referring to here? It is the mistake of assuming oneself to be merely the body. When one realizes the truth of who one truly is through direct experience, it creates a unique state of *Sat-Chit-Ananda*—existence-consciousness-bliss—the bliss of being conscious of one's pristine existence.

This subtle hint from the guru was enough for Eknath to enter a deep state of contemplation. Hence, it is rightly said, "A hint is enough for the wise."

You, too, are given the hint through this example about the importance of concentration.

In worldly life, when we live with unwavering focus, we can attain the highest achievements and reach the pinnacle at every level of life. Then, why not leverage this very concentration to discover our true self, which is the ultimate purpose of life?

The truth is, we do not know who we truly are. Our understanding of who we are is limited to our physical appearance, our body and its name, our relationships with those around us, and our beliefs about ourselves. We have identified ourselves with this false sense of "I" like, "I am a husband," "I am a wife," "I am a Hindu," "I am a Christian," "I am a doctor," "I am a lawyer," and so on. However, this is a mere façade. Beyond these superficial layers, lies a deeper truth. We are not merely the body; we are more than just the body. This body is going to perish someday; it is mortal. It is time to know the one that is eternal, the one that functions through this body and keeps it alive, the one whose existence is all-pervading. That essence is Shiva, without which this body is just a corpse, a lifeless shell. This inner essence, often referred to as the Self, Consciousness, or God, is what truly lives. It is this essence that pulsates within all living beings. It is the life-force that drives every breath and thought. Understanding and realizing this essence and dwelling in it is the ultimate purpose of human life.

God has blessed us with the gift of virtues to know this essence. However, after arriving in this world, we get so engrossed in it that we forget to use the virtues we were graced with. Concentration is one such virtue that we are blessed with that can be harnessed to know who we truly are.

You may have observed a small child playing alone. Lost in their own joy, they play with their toys with intense focus. Engrossed in their own world, they carry out all their activities with total concentration. Whether playing, eating, or drawing, they remain completely oblivious to their surroundings. They are connected to their true self.

As they grow up, the allurements around them disrupt and diminish their concentration. It is now time to rekindle this quality from our childhood and strive to know ourselves by immersing ourselves in it. Meditation is one such path that allows us to focus and take the first step toward self-discovery.

Meditation marks the beginning of true knowledge and understanding. While we gain vast knowledge and information throughout our lives, no one has provided the most profound knowledge of knowing our true selves or accessing our inner core. Even if we gained some wisdom from ancient scriptures, though profound, it is often incomplete or fragmented, as their meaning and relevance have changed over time.

To realize this wisdom through our own experience, we must work on our concentration skills. This will allow us to attain that ultimate experience by immersing ourselves in meditation with complete focus. In other words, we should direct our concentration toward achieving the real purpose of Earth-life. The next chapter will provide us with insights and practices into this meditation.

21

Understanding True Meditation

With concentration, you connect with
the inexhaustible reservoir of eternal power,
the source from which the entire universe has originated.

~ Anonymous

As we approach the end of this book, having worked on our concentration, let's delve into the ultimate purpose of meditation. While meditation helps improve our ability to concentrate, it is much more than just focusing the mind. Meditation involves unifying our thoughts, emotions, senses, and mind by directing our attention inward.

There are two categories of meditation:

1. The first category is practiced to enhance concentration, develop skills and qualities, and acquire occult powers, thereby improving the overall quality and productivity of our work.
2. The second category is practiced to know who we truly are, our true self. When we begin this inward journey, we transcend our thoughts and experience profound inner peace and bliss.

Concentration of the mind is crucial in both categories of meditation. The mind, being fickle by nature, is constantly restless. Just as *Yoga* and *Pranayama* are exercises for the body, concentration serves as a vital exercise for the mind.

When the mind is engrossed in too many thoughts, it becomes gross and bloated. Such a mind lacks sensitivity and cannot delve deep into any topic. During meditation, when the mind is focused on a single point, it becomes more subtle and lean. While the mind may initially resist this, gradually it becomes stable. The stable mind then becomes a catalyst in progressing deeper in meditation. Therefore, we must leverage the benefits of concentration for both kinds of meditation.

Mediation is also practiced to fulfill worldly pursuits and cultivate virtues. We practiced Relaxation meditation and Reverse Counting meditation to restore our body's depleted energy. These techniques help us relax both our mind and body, while nurturing our inner qualities.

Concentration of the mind is essential for achieving anything in the external world. A focused mind is necessary even for studying. Concentration boosts our memory power and curbs mental distractions. Meditation increases our ability to focus. For instance, as we have seen earlier, Tratak meditation teaches us the art of single-pointed focus and is designed to cultivate focus. This gradually improves our concentration, enabling us to navigate the external world more effectively.

Some people meditate to attain occult powers, while others meditate to awaken their *Kundalini* (divine energy). Some meditate for healing, while others gain health through Reiki meditation. Essentially, all these techniques help us achieve our goals. Each one may have different goals, but concentration is the path that leads to our destination.

Furthermore, the highest purpose of human life is to know who we truly are through direct experience. For this, the seeker embarks on an inward journey to discover their true essence. After realizing their true self, they experience eternal bliss and peace. Their mind becomes calm and stable. Although they continue to perform the same actions as before, only divine qualities are expressed through them. Just as a ceiling fan's central rod remains steady while the blades spin, after self-realization, the mind remains stable, thoughts no longer entangle, and an effortless divine expression of the Self is enacted through the body.

After realizing our true self, we express divine qualities such as love, joy, peace, and creativity through our feelings, thoughts, speech, and actions, which align with our ultimate goal. Anger, hatred, and malice are not attributes of the Self; they are traits of the ego.

Actually, achieving concentration in meditation is the path, not the destination. By walking this path of disciplined focus and concentration, we can easily reach our ultimate destination of knowing our true self.

For instance, we polish our shoes and keep them ready before stepping out. Similarly, in meditation, we first work on honing our concentration and steadying our mind, so that we can experience our true self.

Unless our mind achieves focus, it will repeatedly stray into thoughts, even during meditation. Such a mind needs to be trained and directed on the path of self-realization.

There are different meditations for this, such as "Self-enquiry Meditation," "Self-observation Meditation," "Thoughtless-state Meditation," and so on. These meditations guide us to a higher state of being, which is the ultimate purpose of life.

To delve deeper into the journey of meditation, you can read the book, *You Are Meditation* by Sirshree. You can also listen to Sirshree's guided meditations on YouTube. You can access these resources by scanning the QR codes given below.

You Are Meditation

Guided Meditation on YouTube

APPENDICES

Appendix A

Breath Control Meditation

A 2016 study revealed that the brainstem, the posterior region of the brain connected to the spinal cord, contains a complex network of neurons that links breathing to the brain. This neural network, known as the "breathing pacemaker," generates the rhythmic pattern of neural activity responsible for breathing.

The brainstem region not only controls the physical act of breathing but also directly communicates with brain areas involved in arousal, attention, and emotion. When we breathe slowly, the signals in this circuit decrease, leading to a more relaxed and less emotionally reactive state. As a result, we can easily distance ourselves from our emotional state or flow of thoughts. However, researchers acknowledge that the exact mechanisms underlying this phenomenon are not yet fully understood.

Yet another study by researchers at the Trinity College Institute of Neuroscience in Dublin has revealed that our breathing patterns are directly linked to our brain's focus network. When we regulate the rhythm of our breathing, particularly through slow-paced breathing, our brain releases a hormone-neurotransmitter called norepinephrine. This hormone activates the brain and body, signalling, "This is important; pay attention." Consequently, our concentration, arousal, alertness, and memory function increase, and we feel more motivated.

When norepinephrine levels in the brain decrease, coupled with an increase in depression, it can worsen ADHD (Attention Deficit

Hyperactivity Disorder), leading to greater challenges with attention and managing hyperactivity. This situation can worsen significantly in homes with a stressful environment, and for children facing excessive academic pressure.

Researchers suggest that norepinephrine helps in the formation of new memories and maintaining brain health. The easiest way to maintain a balanced level of this hormone is through breathing exercises, particularly *Pranayama*. This allows us to focus our attention on our desired direction, whether we are in college, taking an exam, at the office, in a meeting, or any other setting, and no one will even notice.

Breathing exercises offer numerous benefits, including improved alertness, concentration, and enhanced memory. Let's explore how to practice these exercises effectively.

Box breathing technique

The first method is box breathing, also known as the *Samavritti* Pranayama. *Sama* signifies calmness and balance. When the mind is calm, it can fully concentrate. Box breathing is a simple yet highly effective method to enhance concentration. This method is so effective that it is even taught in the United States Navy SEAL training to help maintain focus in intense combat situations.

Box breathing involves four equal phases of breathing. Maintain correct body posture during these practices, as body posture plays a significant role here. So let's understand how to practice this exercise.

1. Sit comfortably, making sure that your neck, back, and shoulders are relaxed, and the spine is erect.
2. Lift your chin slightly so that it is parallel to the ground, keep your neck straight, and open your shoulders so that you don't droop.
3. Once you are comfortable, start inhaling calmly. Breathe in for a count of 4. While you inhale, begin by filling your

lower abdomen, then expand your ribs and lungs, and finally your chest.

4. Take a deep breath for four seconds, allowing each part of your body to expand.
5. Now, hold your breath for four seconds.
6. While exhaling, reverse the process: first empty the chest, then the lungs, and finally the abdomen.
7. And then exhale for four seconds. Once you exhale, hold for four seconds.

This completes one cycle. It is ideal to complete 12 rounds of this cycle every morning. It takes about 192 seconds to complete one set of 12 cycles, i.e., 3 minutes 12 seconds.

Here are some practical tips to ensure you practice this correctly and effectively.

- Initially, pay attention to your face and overall posture to sense any tension or fatigue. Shift your focus to the thought: "I am very calm and relaxed, breathing comfortably, and everything is happening naturally with immense love and care."
- As you progress, gradually increase the duration of each breath by one second. Inhale and exhale so softly that even the person sitting next to you won't notice. The more control you have over your abdomen while breathing, the deeper and calmer your practice will be. Aim for 12 rounds every morning to experience the profound benefits of this practice.

Alternate nostril breathing

Alternate nostril breathing, also known as *Nadi Shodhana Pranayama or Anulom Vilom,* is another effective Pranayama technique. This practice is particularly beneficial for those who struggle with work stress, dwell on the past, or feel overwhelmed by negative thoughts. Practicing this Pranayama strengthens the muscles of the heart and lungs, and also the brain, allowing you to experience mental peace and balanced energy. Additionally, it revitalizes the nervous system, enhancing concentration.

Following are the steps to practice this Pranayama:

1. Sit comfortably with your spine erect and close your eyes.
2. Place the index finger and middle finger of your right hand in the middle of your forehead and close the right nostril of your nose with the thumb, adopting the posture for Pranayama.
3. Exhale slowly through the left nostril.
4. Once you exhale completely, inhale deeply through the left nostril, filling your lungs as much as possible, and hold your breath for a few seconds.
5. Now, switch sides by closing your left nostril with the help of your ring finger and exhale slowly through the right nostril.
6. Once you exhale completely, inhale through the right nostril. Hold your breath for a few seconds and then exhale through the left nostril.

This completes one set of this Pranayama. In this way, practice at least 11 sets of this Pranayama. After you finish, remain in the same posture for a few minutes and feel the calmness.

Just as yoga is an exercise for the body, Pranayama is an exercise for the breath. It increases the flow of vital energy within the body and promotes a cheerful and serene mind. Such a mind is ideal for cultivating focus.

Appendix B

Japanese Secret of Concentration

In 2010, Harvard University conducted a study with 2250 subjects, checking with them at random times (via a phone app) to record what they were doing at that moment and what their mind was focused on. The research revealed that around 47% of the time, the subjects were not paying attention to what was right in front of them. They spent this time daydreaming. Further, the study also states that a wandering mind is not a happy mind, as not being in the present moment was the cause of reported unhappiness, and not the consequence. Thus, the more the mind wanders, the unhappier we become. As per Zen philosophy, "The one whose mind keeps wandering remains unhappy."

On average, a person has about 50,000 to 60,000 thoughts each day. Considering that a person is awake for 16 hours daily, they experience approximately 5 thoughts every 4 seconds, which means each thought lasts less than a second!

Further, the study also states that nearly 90% of our thoughts are from the past. And often, the same kind of thoughts persist and bother us for years. In psychological terms, it is called the brain's Default Mode Network. This network is active when we are not engaged in externally oriented or goal-directed activities. This state limits our ability to stay mindful or focused.

In his book, "Zen Mind, Beginner's Mind," renowned author Shunryu Suzuki says, "When you do anything with complete stillness and presence, your true nature emerges." Zen philosophy emphasizes mindfulness, focusing entirely on what is happening at this very moment and nothing else. For example, when you sit, just sit, or when you eat, just eat. In other words, whatever you are doing, simply do that. Without dwelling on the past or dreaming about the future, concentrate on the present moment—right here, right now.

Shunryu Suzuki also shares some simple techniques for boosting concentration. They are so easy that anyone can practice them. Additionally, we can practice them while working. Furthermore, they can help us complete our tasks more quickly and efficiently.

These exercises are as follows:

1. **Awareness of the body:** Maintaining proper body posture is crucial for preventing discomfort. First, pay attention to your physical posture. If you slouch while sitting, adjust your posture so that your spine is in an erect position. An improper physical posture can decrease your awareness and cause your mind to wander.

2. **Breathing:** Our breath is like a swing that flows intuitively in and out, uninterrupted. When we focus on our breath for just a few seconds, our mind naturally shifts to the present, enhances our focus, and offers an immediate sense of calm and peace. This calmness represents true concentration.

3. **The vast mind:** Imagine your mind as an empty road, with different vehicles moving along that road representing various thoughts passing through your mind. You are standing on the balcony of your apartment, which symbolizes the balcony of your awareness, observing these vehicles, or thoughts, as they pass by. Do not try to stop or board any of them, and refrain from commenting on them, such as saying, "This vehicle is good, this is bad," or "Why do I see such vehicles?" In essence, avoid wandering around the world with any thought, and do not judge any of them as good or bad. Soon, you will notice that the traffic

of thoughts has decreased, and your mind has become empty. This state is referred to as a vast mind. In this state, the brain functions at its most natural and effortless pace, making concentration easier. This practice is very effective in developing self-awareness.

4. **Self-awareness:** Our mind cannot stay calm for too long. Thoughts keep arising one after another. Self-awareness is being aware of our own thoughts and knowing them without any judgment or bias. This final practice is essential for developing concentration.

Those who try to concentrate or meditate often become frustrated when their mind wanders frequently. This is a common experience for beginners. Our mind is like a small child. We cannot force it to do anything, but we can gently and lovingly pursue it to do something that can calm it down. If your mind wanders frequently, bring it back to the present moment with awareness, tenderness, and great love. This way, you can practice concentration without feeling frustrated.

Appendix C

Concentration - a Survey

Studies back in the 1990s suggested that our alertness cycles naturally vary, restricting our attention span to approximately 90 minutes. We need a 15-minute break to restore optimal focus levels.

With the advent of technology, growing dependence on AI, the ever-increasing deluge of content on social media, and the demands of a fast-paced virtual environment, our attention spans have shrunk significantly. This is a serious concern.

Another study found that ever since smartphones became widely available, the average attention span has notably decreased in recent years. In 2000, it was approximately 12 seconds, but by 2013, it had dropped to just 8 seconds.

Many of us frequently check our mobile phones several times, not just during the day but even during the wee hours. According to a 2016 survey conducted by Deloitte, more than 40% of individuals admit to scrolling through their phones within five minutes of waking up, while 48% even wake up in the middle of the night to check their screens.

As per the data, Millennials (born 1981-1996) and Gen Z (born 1997-2012) spend almost two or more hours on their smartphones during work hours for non-work-related activities. Even Gen Alphas (born 2013-Present) spend nearly three or more hours on screens. Nowadays, many people rarely turn off their phones.

Mobile users who frequently use their phones tend to leave a web page within just 10 to 20 seconds, quickly jumping to look for something else due to a diminished attention span.

Common signs of difficulty in focusing include:

1. Unexplained frustration or anger
2. Increased distractions, anxiety, and restlessness
3. Struggling to remain still in one place
4. Troubled by constantly racing thoughts
5. Increased irritability
6. A sense of hopelessness and frustration
7. Memory problems, forgetting even the most basic things

Following are some of the psychological reasons that can contribute to difficulty in concentrating:

1. **Inability to focus:** This problem is commonly found in children and, to some extent, in adults as well, which can significantly impact their productivity at home, school, or work.
2. **Depression:** Depression is a mental disorder characterized by a persistent feeling of sadness, hopelessness, and a loss of interest in everyday activities for a prolonged period. As a result, it can be challenging to organize our thoughts.
3. **Deep shock:** Experiencing deep trauma after the death of a loved one can take months to overcome grief.
4. **Anxiety:** Individuals experiencing severe anxiety frequently find it challenging to concentrate on one task due to their attention being divided among numerous distractions.
5. **Mood swings:** Uncontrollable mental states, such as bipolar disorder*, can involve persistent racing thoughts.

**Bipolar disorder is a mental health condition characterized by mood swings from one extreme to another. During a manic episode, a person experiences an extremely high mood with lots of energy (feeling very happy, excited, overactive).*

6. **Medical conditions:** We can have difficulty concentrating due to underlying medical conditions.
    - **Hormonal issues:** Dysfunction of the adrenal glands can lead to changes in our energy levels and our ability to concentrate
    - **Thyroid issues:** An overactive or underactive thyroid gland can affect our concentration.
    - **A deficiency of red blood cells:** Red blood cells transport oxygen to the brain, and their deficiency can deprive the brain of the vital energy necessary for proper functioning.

Environmental Factors

Changes caused by certain lifestyle habits or events can impact our ability to concentrate.

1. **Stress:** Stress can disrupt our focus, making it harder to complete tasks, and this can lead to a chronic condition.
2. **Stimulating environment:** When a task seems uninteresting, it can become extremely challenging to turn off the TV, put aside the cell phone, or stop chatting with colleagues.
3. **Lack of sleep:** After a tough day at work, quality sleep is crucial for the body's overall fitness. When the body is fatigued, exhaustion naturally leads to slumber. Insufficient sleep can significantly impact our physical and mental well-being.
4. **Burnout:** When we are on the brink of emotional exhaustion, we feel drained even before attempting to focus on any task.
5. **Old age:** It is normal to occasionally forget words or misplace things like keys as we age. Although this can cause some inconvenience, it generally does not require treatment.

These symptoms significantly impact our daily routine, strain our relationships, and make work feel overwhelming.

Here is a quick recap of techniques to improve our concentration:

1. Enhance focus by engaging in certain brain exercises or games.
2. Adopt a personalized approach to train the brain.
3. Improve the quality of sleep.
4. Dedicate time to exercise.
5. Take time to connect with nature.
6. Practice meditation.
7. Take regular breaks.
8. Listen to music.
9. Cultivate perseverance

Lastly, perseverance is the key. Whenever you feel tempted to quit, push yourself to continue for just five more minutes, by simply saying, "Just five more minutes..., just five more repetitions of this exercise..., or just five more lines to read..." This will help boost your focus and overcome frustration. This approach is not only a training technique but also a powerful method for accomplishing goals.

At first glance, sitting still may seem easy; however, it is challenging. Practice siting still for 5 minutes, without moving or doing anything, to pause between tasks. If you already practice meditation, combine it with mindful breathing, and let your breath be the anchor to this stillness.

◆◆◆

You can mail your opinion or feedback on this book to:
books.feedback@tejgyan.org

About Sirshree

Sirshree's spiritual quest, which began during his childhood, led him on a journey through various schools of philosophy and meditation practices. He studied a wide range of literature on mind science and spirituality. After a long period of deep contemplation on the truth of life, his quest culminated in attaining the ultimate truth.

Sirshree espouses, "All spiritual paths that lead to the truth begin differently but culminate at the same point – Understanding. This understanding is complete in itself. Listening to this understanding is enough to attain the Truth." Over the last two decades, he has dedicated his life to raise mass consciousness.

Sirshree has delivered more than 4000 discourses that throw light on this understanding. He has designed a system for wisdom, which makes it accessible to all. This system has inspired people from all walks of life to progress on their journey of the Truth. Thousands of seekers join in a virtual prayer for World Peace and Global Healing daily at 9:09 am and 9:09 pm.

About Tej Gyan Foundation

Tej Gyan Foundation is a non-profit organization founded on the teachings of Sirshree. The Foundation disseminates Tejgyan – the wisdom that guides one from self-development to Self-realization, leading towards Self-stabilization.

The Foundation's system for imparting wisdom has been assessed by international quality auditors and accredited with the ISO 9001:2015 certification. This wisdom has been presented in a simple, systematic, and practically applicable form that makes it accessible to people from all walks of life, regardless of religion, caste, social strata, country, or belief system.

The Foundation has centers in more than 400 cities and towns across India and other countries. The mission of Tej Gyan Foundation is to create a highly evolved society by leading seekers from negative thoughts to positive thoughts and further, from positive thoughts to Happy thoughts. A 'Happy thought' is the auspicious thought of being free from all thoughts, leading to the state of supreme bliss beyond thoughts.

If you seek such wisdom that leads you beyond mere knowledge, dissolves all problems, frees you from all limiting beliefs, reveals the true nature of divinity, and establishes you in the ultimate truth, then it is time to discover Tejgyan; it is time to rise above the mundane knowledge of words and experience Tejgyan!

The MahaAasmani Magic of Awakening Retreat

Self-development to Self-realization towards Self-stabilization

Do you wish to experience unconditional happiness that is not dependent on any reason? Happiness that is permanent and only increases with time? Do you wish to experience love, peace, self-belief, harmony in relationships, prosperity, and true contentment? Do you wish to progress in all facets of your life, viz. physical, mental, social, financial, and spiritual?

If you seek answers to these questions and are thirsty for the ultimate truth, then you are welcome to participate in the MahaAasmani Magic of Awakening retreat organized by Tej Gyan Foundation. This is the Foundation's flagship retreat based on the teachings of Sirshree.

The purpose of this retreat

The purpose of this retreat is that every human being should:

- Discover the answer to "Who am I" and "Why am I?" through direct experience and be established in ultimate bliss.
- Learn the art of living in the present, free from the burden of the past and the anxiety of the future.
- Acquire practical tools to help quieten the chattering mind and dissolve problems.
- Discover missing links in the practices of Meditation (*Dhyana*), Action (*Karma*), Wisdom (*Gyana*), and Devotion (*Bhakti*).

SELECT BOOKS AUTHORED BY SIRSHREE

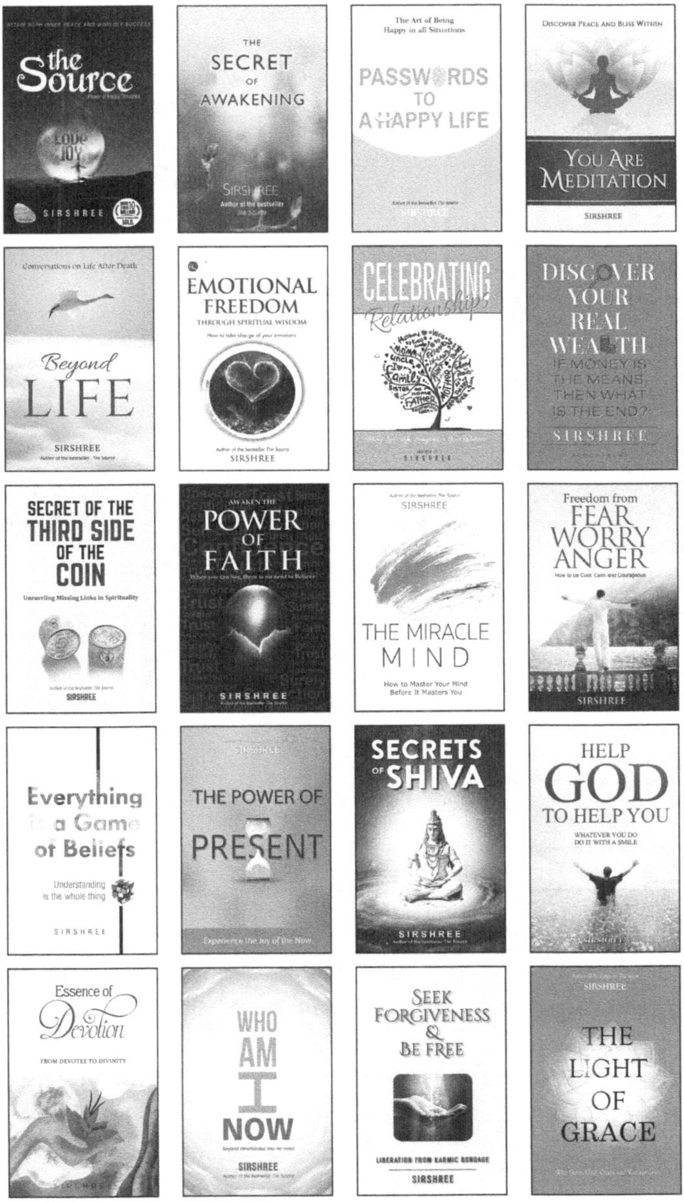

To order these and other books authored by Sirshree

Visit www.gethappythoughts.org

Tej Gyan Foundation – Contact details

Registered Office:
Happy Thoughts Building, Vikrant Complex, Near Tapovan Mandir, Pimpri, Pune 411017, INDIA. Contact: +91 20-27411240, +91 20-27412576

MaNaN Ashram:
Survey No. 43, Sanas Nagar, Nandoshi Gaon, Kirkatwadi Phata, Off Sinhagad Road, Taluka Haveli, Pune district - 411024, INDIA. Contact: +91 992100 8060.

WORLD PEACE PRAYER

Divine Light of Love, Bliss, and Peace is Showering;
The Golden Light of Higher Consciousness is Rising;
All negativity on Earth is Dissolving;
Everyone is in Peace and Blissfully Shining;
O God, Gratitude for Everything!

Members of Tej Gyan Foundation have been offering this impersonal mass prayer for many years. Those who are happy can offer this prayer. Those feeling low or suffering from illness can receive healing with this prayer.

If you are feeling troubled or sick, please sit to receive the healing effect of this prayer. Visualize that the divine white healing light is being showered on earth through the prayers of thousands and is also reaching you, bringing you peace and good health. You can dwell in this feeling for some time and then offer your gratitude to those offering the prayer.

A Humble Appeal

More than a million peace lovers pray for World Peace and Global Healing every morning and evening at 9:09. Also, a prayer (in Hindi) to elevate consciousness is webcast every day on YouTube at 3:30 pm and 9:00 pm IST. Please participate in this noble endeavor.

9 788198 925893

Printed at Repro India Ltd.